I FORGOT TO TELL YOU

I Forgot To Tell You

THROUGH THE YEAR (2)

with

ELIZABETH URCH

LOCHALSH PUBLICATIONS
PITLOCHRY

First Published in 2000 by

LOCHALSH PUBLICATIONS
11 Tom-na-Moan Road
Pitlochry
Perthshire
PH16 5HL

A catalogue record for this book is available
from the British Library.

ISBN 1 873891 50 4

Typeset in New Baskerville

Printed in Scotland by
Wm. Culross & Son Ltd.
Queen Street, Coupar Angus, Perthshire PH13 9DF
Tel: 01828 627266 Fax: 01828 627146
ISDN: 01828 628950 E-mail: culross@btinternet.com
www.culross.co.uk

JANUARY

As for the future, your task is not to foresee, but to enable.

St Exupery

January 1st

Johann Christoph Friedrich Von Schiller was a friend of Goethe, and a poet and dramatist. The well-known words of his Ode To Joy are now set to Beethoven's Ninth Choral Symphony for the European Anthem. It was conducted by Leonard Bernstein as Communism visibly collapsed when the wall in Berlin came down in 1989. It became The Ode To Freedom instead.

Other words of his are good ones with which to start any new era, including a New Year, and even a new millennium.

There are three lessons I would write -
Three words as with a golden pen,
In tracings of eternal light
Upon the hearts of men.

HAVE HOPE! Though clouds environ round
And gladness hides her face in scorn
Put thou the shadow from thy brow -
No night but has its morn.

HAVE FAITH! Where'er thy bark is driven,
The calm's disport, the tempest's mirth -
Know this: God rules the host of heaven,
The inhabitants of earth.

HAVE LOVE! Not love alone for one
But man as man thy brother call,
And scatter like the circling sun
Thy charities on all.

Thus grave these words upon thy soul
Hope, faith and love, and thou shalt find
Strength when life's surges maddest roll
Light when thou else wert blind.

January 2nd

Did you know that when an Oriental carpet is woven, a deliberate mistake is woven into the pattern? This is because the weavers are taught, 'Only Allah is perfect.'

Every day is revered in memory of some Saint and today Gregory of Nazianzen is remembered as a colleague of Basil the Great. Both studied at Athens University in the early 4th century. Gregory felt himself unworthy to be a Bishop, and wrote words which are similar to the Oriental carpet weavers. 'Let it be assured that to do no wrong is really superhuman and belongs to God alone.' Gregory said one could only aim at perfection by becoming a friend of God. As we leave behind last year's shortcomings, let us remember that God is merciful.

January 3rd

Billy Connelly said his father used to declare: 'Everybody makes mistakes. That's why they put rubbers on the ends of pencils.'

January 4th

McIntosh Patrick, a beloved Scottish artist, on his ninetieth birthday revealed that he had never owned or used a camera. He preferred to paint what he called a living picture. He has told of walking in a lane near his home when a car full of tourists stopped. Not recognising him they said, 'We just had to stop here because this view is so like one of McIntosh Patrick's paintings.'

He said that they had made a serious mistake - they had got things the wrong way round. He would have preferred them to say, 'McIntosh Patrick's paintings are like this beautiful view.' He knew a great deal about a sense of perspective, and not only in art. As Oscar Wilde commented, there are people who know the price of everything and the value of nothing.

January 5th

Oftentimes I have heard you speak of one who commits a wrong as though he were not one of you, but a stranger unto you and an intruder upon your world.

But I say that even as the holy and righteous cannot rise beyond the highest which is in each one of you so the wicked and the weak cannot fall lower than the lowest which is in you also.

And as a single leaf turns not yellow but with the silent knowledge of the whole tree, so the wrong-doer cannot do wrong without the hidden will of you all.

Kahlil Gibran

January 6th

Do not store up for yourselves treasures on earth, where moth and rust destroy, and where thieves break in and steal. But store up for yourselves treasures in heaven, where moth and rust do not destroy, and where moths do not break in and steal. For where your treasure is, there will your heart be also.

Matthew 6: 19-21

January 7th

Lord, we do not want to face the pressures of this opening year alone. We feel the draw of the crowd who would lure us into standards lower than those you have set for us. This fast moving world sometimes bewilders and dismays us. Yet there is excitement and great joy in confronting the future with you as our companion. Come now and dwell within us so that your guidance and direction are ever clear.

January 8th

A former Bishop of Chester tells of his early days in the journey towards becoming an Anglican clergyman. He wasn't sure which of two theological colleges to choose, one being north of the Thames and the other being south. He decided in a haphazard way to let his Bible fall open and see what mighty truth would be revealed to him. So he was overjoyed when he read the words, 'You shall take the north gate.' His bewilderment quickly returned when he explored the situation further and discovered that the theological college north of the Thames was called Southgate. He said he thought God was teasing him for abusing the Scriptures in this way. He soon found out that there are better ways to seek out the will of God, than by a 'lucky dip.'

January 9th

When I was a child, I used to be fascinated by a woman we knew who kept what she called her 'Box of Promises.' She would dip into it daily in a haphazard fashion, and read out a verse of Scripture which was to offer comfort for that day. We could have a dip as well if we happened to be around, and afterwards you might well be given one of those old-time conversation lozenges to pop in your mouth after you had shared its words of wisdom with whoever was around. Though I revelled in these little attentions, I confess to being baffled when I found she was also in the habit of consulting her horoscope in the local rag. I was never quite sure which of these haphazard messages controlled her life, if indeed any of them did.

January 10th

I have on my book shelves a very tattered old copy of a precious classic written early in the twentieth century by Dr. Alexander Irvine. It is called 'My Lady of the Chimney Corner.'

There's a lot of wisdom in it in the words of Anna, Alexander's mother. He calls the book but the torn manuscript of the most beautiful life he ever knew. Anna lived at the bottom of the world in Antrim, which is not many miles from my friend who was devoted to her Box of Promises. If Anna and she had known each other, Anna could well have said to her, 'A ploughman who skims the surface strikes no stones, but it's because he isn't ploughing deep enough.'

January 11th

After what has gone before, the story I now tell you may seem difficult to relate. St Augustine of Hippo lived a life of incontinence and sin, but his mother Monica never gave up praying for him. One day he was weeping under a fig tree as his struggle with the frailties of his life had overcome him. He seemed to hear the voice of a child singing the words, 'Take it and read.' This stemmed his flow of tears and he felt he was listening to a divine command. He seized his Bible and let it fall open at Romans chapter 13 and he read verses 13 and 14.

Not in revelling and drunkenness, not in lust and wantonness, not in quarrels and rivalries.

Rather arm yourself with the Lord Jesus Christ. Spend no more thought on Nature and Nature's appetites.

Augustine's conversion had taken place. God had definitely intervened, but there were so many factors present to enable this haphazard opening of the Scriptures to be effective. There were the circumstances, the prayers of those who loved

Augustine, the inner promptings of Augustine himself all lining up with the vital Scripture, and the promptings of the Holy Spirit.

The more you pray, the more positive coincidences there are. 'God Instances' perhaps.

January 12th

Child to Grandpa: Why are you always reading your Bible?
Grandpa: I'm swotting for my finals!

January 13th

I guide you in the way of wisdom
  and lead you along straight paths
When you walk your steps will not be hampered:
  when you run you will not stumble.
Hold on to instruction, do not let it go;
  guard it well, for it is your life.

Proverbs 4: 11-13

January 14th

Lord, your word teaches that those who are in Christ have died to sin and been raised to new life with Christ.
Forgive me for the many ways in which I remain alive to my sins, and dead to the way of Christ;
for the secret sins which I harbour in my heart, and which no-one knows of but you;
for the open sins which I have become so used to that I no longer try to hide them;
for the shared sins of your church which so often betrays you and its high calling.

Merciful God, as I confess my shortcomings and failures; pardon, forgive and remake me, for the sake of Jesus Christ who died for me and rose again.

Malcolm Ramsay

January 15th

A few years ago I drove with a New Zealand friend along the South shore of Loch Tay. It was a beautiful clear day and as we traversed this tortuous hilly road we stopped often at the viewpoints to savour the spectacular views of Ben Lawers, the highest mountain in Perthshire, and the waters of the loch with its crannog, as well as enjoying the nearby delights of wild flowers and heathers.

When we reached the Falls of Dochart at Killin on the western extremity of the loch, I stopped the car and we spread out a large map of the area to study the way we had travelled and to decide which of several scenic routes we would use to continue our outing. An American drew up alongside and asked if he could study the map with us. He had come by the same tortuous but beautiful road which had so filled us with delight, and when he discovered that I lived in the area, he said, 'Perhaps you will put in a word to the appropriate quarter, on behalf of visitors like myself, appealing for that road to be made into a dual carriageway. It took ages to negotiate that journey from Kenmore to Killin.'

I was lost for words. We had travelled the same road. We were at exactly the same destination. But I felt we were a million miles apart. Then I pointed out to him that there was a road on the North shore of the loch which he could have used - still interesting, less tortuous, but what views he would have missed. Well, I guess he missed them anyway!

When I have been travelling along the sometimes tortuous uphill road of life, with the journey needing great care, I remind myself of that conversation. I tell myself I must take time to stop at the viewpoints for it would be so easy in my frustration to miss them. We cannot always choose a different, easier road, but perhaps if we could we would miss something of infinite beauty and we would lose that wonderful experience of being 'surprised by joy.'

> Two roads diverged in a wood, and I -
> I took the one less travelled by,
> And that made all the difference.

Robert Frost

January 16th

There are two Greek words that can be interpreted as 'time.' 'Chronos' is time that can be measured as with a clock or a calendar. 'Kairos' is time filled with opportunity and some kind of spiritual presence. Time is such a strange thing. When nothing special is happening, it seems to drag on endlessly and we say, 'That seemed like an eternity.' When it is crevassed with sorrow or draped with joy, we often say, 'Time stood still.' In fact, I think we are getting our statements the wrong way round. When sorrow and joy intervene, time takes on a new aspect and becomes part of eternity.

January 17th

To see a world in a grain of sand
And a heaven in a wild flower
Hold infinity in the palm of your hand
And eternity in an hour.

William Blake

January 18th

What if the road be rough, that might be smooth?
Is not the rough road best for you, until
You learn by patient walking in the truth
To trust and hope in God, and to be still.

Walter Chalmers Smith

January 19th

Jeffrey Barnard was a dissolute alcoholic journalist, who, with his great aptitude for pertinent comment, said as his life dragged on, 'I think I'm going to surprise God by being late, just as hitherto I have always been punctual for the devil.'

January 20th

A Time For Everything

There is a time for everything, and a season for every activity under heaven:

a time to be born and a time to die,
a time to plant and a time to uproot,
a time to kill and a time to heal,
a time to tear down and a time to build,
a time to weep and a time to laugh,
a time to mourn and a time to dance,
a time to scatter stones and a time to gather them,
a time to embrace and a time to refrain,
a time to search and a time to give up,
a time to keep and a time to throw away,
a time to tear and a time to mend,
a time to be silent and a time to speak,
a time to love and a time to hate,
a time for war and a time for peace.

Ecclesiastes 3: 1-8

January 21st

A Motorist's Prayer

Grant to me a road and a watchful eye
That none may suffer harm as I pass by
Thou givest life - I pray no act of mine
May take away, or mar that gift of thine.
Shield those, dear Lord, who bear me company
From fools and fire and all calamity.
Teach me to use my car for others' need.
Nor miss through lack of wit, or love of speed
The beauties of thy world, that thus I may
With joy and courtesy go on my way.

Unattributed

January 22nd

Somebody once asked C.S. Lewis to define a practising Christian and if there were any other variety. Of course there are many who claim only to be nominal Christians distinguishing themselves only as not being a Buddhist or a Hindu but without claiming any close allegiance with Christ.

The word Christian is not often mentioned in the New Testament but we are specifically told in Acts 11: 26 that the disciples were first called Christians at Antioch. The word Christian only appears in two other places in the New Testament. Agrippa in Acts 26: 28 may have used it sarcastically and in 1 Peter 4: 14-16 it is a term of reproach which may have been meant to be derogatory. But though in the first instance it was used with scorn, by the end of the first century the Christians themselves accepted the name as indicating something of God's glory.

C.S. Lewis answered his questioner by saying that a practising Christian refers every single act, feeling, experience, pleasant or otherwise, to God in Christ. Though they say that practice makes perfect, we have still a long way to go, have we not? As someone has said, if we lived in the age when people were arrested for being Christians, would there be enough evidence to convict us?

January 23rd

I remember struggling in my youth trying to practise Paderewski's Minuet. I was interested not only in this piece that he had composed, but also in the fact that when he wasn't being

Prime Minister of Poland, he was touring, playing his own and others' compositions. My music master told me that before he died in New York in 1941 he had suffered a period when he was criticised for losing quality of tone and Paderewski himself had said, 'If I stop practising for a day, I myself know the difference in the quality of my playing. If I stop for a couple of days, my family will comment on the differences. When I stop for three or four days, my friends will notice. When I stop for a week, then the world will surely know.'

How apt that we should apply those words to ourselves, if we are trying to 'practise the presence of Christ' as Brother Lawrence referred to it.

January 24th

'I know a great deal of Greek and Latin learning. I have still to learn even the alphabet of how to be a saint.

Arsenius (5th century)

January 25th

A Scot who continually declared himself an irreligious man, was one day stranded on a mountain, and looking helplessly into emptiness with no prospect of early rescue. When finally he was brought by the Mountain Rescue Team to safety, someone asked him if he had prayed at any time when he was lost. Gruffly, he admitted that he had, and then said, 'Well, who else was there to appeal to? I could hardly ask my MP!'

January 26th

The Agnostic

No matter how I probe and prod
I cannot quite believe in God.
But oh! I hope to God that He
Unswervingly believes in me.

E.Y.Harburg

When C.S. Lewis at last gave up his atheism and agnosticism and acknowledged that God was God, he said that he must have been the most reluctant and dejected convert ever. But he came to see what he thought should have been obvious earlier, that the Divine humility will accept a convert even on such terms. 'The hardness of God is kinder than the softness of man, and his compulsion is our liberation.'

January 27th

The law of the Lord is perfect
 reviving the soul,
The statutes of the Lord are trustworthy
 making wise the simple.
The precepts of the Lord are right
 giving joy to the heart
The commandments of the Lord are radiant
 giving light to the eyes.
The fear of the Lord is pure,
 enduring for ever.
The ordinances of the Lord are sure
 and altogether righteous.
They are more precious than gold,
 than much pure gold;
They are sweeter than honey,
 than honey from the comb.
By them is your servant warned;
 in keeping them there is great reward.

Psalm 19: 7-11

January 28th

Lord, you offer us your protection: but like a wayward child refusing his father's hand when crossing a dangerous road, we pretend we can manage on our own.
Lord, you offer us your strength: but like a disheartened invalid, tossing and restless in his weakness, we push away the support of a caring friend.
Lord, you offer to help us understand: but like a malicious slanderer, we prefer at times the pleasure of finding out that our fellows possess feet of clay.
Lord, you offer us justice: but we choose at times to wallow in the glee of seeing an opponent get his come-uppance.

Lord God, we are sorry for our rebellion
 We accept your eternal protection
 Your offer of strength
 The light of your understanding
 Your unfailing justice.
But most of all, we accept your gifts of
 Love, Peace and Forgiveness.

January 29th

All over Scotland at this time of year, people are attending Burns suppers, eating haggis and reciting Burns' poems. Some years back, Sir Alec Douglas-Home was a guest and was sitting beside the Bishop of Dunkeld. Sir Alec said he was very surprised that the Bishop had not been asked to say the Grace before the meal. 'Oh, I was asked,' said the Bishop, 'but I didn't want the Lord to know that this is the kind of convivial company I sometimes keep.'

January 30th

When Rabbie Burns was on a visit to St. Mary's Isle, the Earl of Selkirk asked him to say Grace. He obeyed in the words of what is now known as The Selkirk Grace.

> Some ha'e meat, and canna eat,
> And some wad eat that want it;
> But we ha'e meat and we can eat
> And sae the Lord be thankit.

January 31st

As we close this first month of this new year let us move into the next with this Celtic blessing.

> Be a guiding star above me
> Illuminate each rock and tide
> Guide my ship across the waters
> To the waveless harbourside.

FEBRUARY

So rolls the changing year, and so we change
Motion so swift, we know not that we move.

D.M. Craik

February 1st

SLOW US DOWN, O LORD

O Heavenly Father, recall to our minds your great goodness
Rekindle our hearts with love.
Make us willing and bold to draw near to you in prayer
And … slow us down, Lord.

Ease the pounding of our hearts by the quieting of our mind,
Steady our hurried pace with the vision of the Eternal reach of time,
Give us, amid the confusion of the day, the everlasting hills.
Break the tensions of our nerves and muscles with the soothing music
Of the singing streams that live in our memory.

Help us to know the magical restoring power of sleep.
Teach us the art of taking minute vacations,
Of slowing down to look at a flower,
To chat with a friend, to pat a dog,
To read a few lines from a good book.

Remind us each day of the fable of the hare and the tortoise,
That we may know that the race is not always to the swift.
Help us to know that there is more to life than increasing the speed.

Let us look upwards to the branches of the towering oak.
It grew slowly and well … SLOW US DOWN, O LORD …
Inspire us to send our roots deep into the soul of life's enduring values
And then help us to grow towards the stars of our greater destiny.
In your mercy, save us from the temptations that often beset us
And bring us to Eternal life by the power of your Holy Spirit.

Unattributed

February 2nd

A lecturer of medical students was talking to them about the modern prevalence of stress and strain, and the need on many occasions for a doctor to prescribe rest. He said, 'I'm afraid that most of these extended periods of rest are Sundays in arrears.' If we find in our lives that the only time we have for stillness and quietness is the period set aside for sleep, then we need to look again at the pattern of our lives.

The old Jewish teachers taught that six days a week the people should pray, 'Lord bless our going out and our coming in,' but on the seventh they should pray, 'Spread over us the shelter of your peace.' In the wonderful carcadian rhythms which affect the living things in our planet, the rhythm of one day's rest in seven seems to have been peculiarly bestowed on man. We ignore this at our peril.

February 3rd

One summer Saturday evening I was on the island of Vårdö, one of the Åland Islands. At six o'clock the church bells started to ring out and I asked if this meant a wedding or a funeral. 'Oh no,' my companion replied, 'That is simply to remind us that tomorrow is the Lord's Day, and we should now cease our work and prepare for the day of rest and worship.'

Nearer to my home there is an old kirk in a village where there has been Christian worship for many centuries. The old church has been rebuilt several times, and until it ceased to be used a decade or so ago, the church bells rang out on a Sunday morning one hour ahead of the worship service to remind the farming community that it was time to leave the chores and prepare and change garb for attendance in the Lord's House.

There is another very old church some miles away, built on a height. There is only one service there annually, but when you stand outside the church you can see for miles around the old drove roads, where the congregation travelled to fulfil their obligation of worship. Of course the Industrial Revolution changed life dramatically, but it would be good if we could ponder again the words in Genesis telling us that God rested on and blessed the seventh day and made it holy. We should be able in good conscience to offer up our rest to him in worship, just as we often offer up our work.

February 4th

I remember when I was a child being told the story of an Ulster Scot whose family were very strict Sabbatarians. He became an atheist later in life and boasted that he had thus cast off the restraints of his childhood, but his friends and neighbours were amused by one eccentricity.

When he went out to do a bit of gardening on a Sunday, he always changed from his workaday gardening togs into a more respectable garb.

Quite recently I heard a Dundee man reminiscing about his childhood, when if his father had to use his hammer for any purpose on a Sunday, his mother insisted that it should be wrapped in a thick sock so that the Sabbath calm should not be disturbed by the noise.

February 5th

There was a woman on one of our islands where the keeping of a day of rest has come to be a burden rather than a re-creation, which I think might be the full purpose and need of that special day. Everything, but everything was 'Thou shalt not' on this day, without discriminating as to what activity might be wholesome and what might be best done without. A younger relative remonstrated with her, reminding her that Christ himself walked through the cornfields on the Sabbath, and when he picked corn he was rebuked by the Pharisees.

'Well,' said the old lady, 'I dinnae think ony the better o' the Lord for daein' a thing like that.'

February 6th

He who dwells in the shelter of the Most High
 will rest in the shadow of the Almighty.
I will say of the Lord, He is my refuge and my fortress,
 my God, in whom I trust.

Surely he will save you from the fowler's snare
 and from the deadly pestilence.
He will cover you with his feathers,
 and under his wings you will find refuge
 his faithfulness will be your shield and rampart.

You will not fear the terror of night,
nor the arrow that flies by day,
nor the pestilence that stalks in the darkness
nor the plague that destroys at midday.

For he will command his angels concerning you
to guard you in all your ways.

Psalm 91: 1-6 & 9

February 7th

Dear Lord and Father of mankind
Forgive our foolish ways!
Reclothe us in our rightful mind:
In purer lives your service find,
In deeper reverence praise.

Drop your still dews of quietness
Till all our strivings cease
Take from our lives the strain and stress,
And let our ordered lives confess
The beauty of your peace.

John Greenleaf Whittier

February 8th

One Sunday I was passing through a city in the Midlands and went into a church service which happily and unusually was packed out with young families. I sat up in the gallery and heard and saw very clearly the reactions of this lively congregation. When the vicar started his sermon which was for all the family, he said, 'Hands up anyone who has never told a lie.' Only one hand went up - it belonged to a young lad of about eight years old. Suddenly another lad sitting quite near reached forward and pulled down the upraised hand. I discovered later that this self-appointed moralist was an older brother! The already relaxed congregation went on to hear a memorable sermon on falling short of perfection, but the point had already been unwittingly made by this little living parable.

February 9th

Man is the only animal that blushes. Or needs to.

Mark Twain

February 10th

They do not lie;
They just neglect to tell the truth.
They do not take;
They simply cannot bring themselves to give.
They do not steal;
They scavenge.
They will not rock the boat;
But did you ever see them pull an oar?
They will not pull you down;
They simply let you pull them up,
And let that pull you down.
They do not hurt you;
They merely will not help you.
They do not hate you;
They merely cannot love you.
They will not burn you;
They'll only fiddle while you burn.
They are the Nothing People;
The sins-of omission folk;
The neither-good-nor bad
And therefore - worse.
Because the good at least keep busy trying
And the bad try just as hard.
Both have that character that comes
From caring, action and conviction.
So, give me every time an honest sinner
Or even a saint.
But, God and Satan,
Get together and protect me from
The Nothing People.

Ivan H. Scheier

February 11th

An unusually truthful Secondhand Car Advert:
Peugeot: Red with two shades of rust.
Metro: One careful owner - and six not so careful!

Angels, devils, saints and sinners
Look alike to all beginners
We discover much too late
How to differentiate.

Bonnie Day

February 12th

He that cheats with an oath reveals that he is afraid of the enemy but that he thinks little of God.

Plutarch

When a man takes an oath.....he's holding his own self in his own hands. Like water. And if he opens his fingers - he needn't hope to find himself again.

Robert Bolt

February 13th

Lord, who may dwell in your sanctuary?
  Who may live on your holy hill?
He whose walk is blameless
  and who does what is righteous,
who speaks the truth from his heart
  and has no slander on his tongue,
who does his neighbour no wrong
  and casts no slur on his fellow man,
who despises a vile man
  but honours those that fear the Lord,
who keeps his oath
  even when it hurts,
who lends his money without usury
  and does not accept a bribe against the innocent.

He who does these things will never be shaken.

Psalm 15

February 14th

Lord, you have given us the freedom to choose each day the way of truth or the way of falsehood. Sometimes the choice is so hard. The lie we contemplate may bring us instant gain, and the truth we feel like rejecting may mean we face loss, even grievous loss. But whether it is little or much, help us to trust you to enable us to choose aright. You said if we know the truth, then the truth will make us free. Give us today this true freedom of the soul.

February 15th

Just prior to my husband's death as a young man, we had been told the full truth about the devastating illness which had struck. In great weakness, he asked me to walk with him to the dark cupboard where earlier, when he was stronger, he had placed some bowls of carefully planted bulbs. The green shoots were just appearing. With my help he carried them through to the room where his bed was, and he placed them at vantage points, where day by day he would be able to see the progress of the little snowdrops. They were for us in the days to come - days of agony and distress - symbols of the life eternal, promise of hope for the future.

The tempests of the previous winter had robbed the plants of every bloom, of every leaf. Yet when there seemed nothing left but a bare and desolate little bulb, still within that wizened, brown little scrap there was the material of leaf and flower for a new season. The tempests of sorrow had stripped our lives bare, but we were certain now that the buds of celestial hope would burst forth into flower and bloom again in a better land.

February 16th

The Snowdrop

Close to the sod
There can be seen
A thought of God
In white and green
Unmarred, unsoiled,
It cleft its clay,
Serene, unspoiled,
It views the day

It is so holy
And yet so lowly
Would you enjoy
Its grace and dower
And not destroy
The living flower?
Then you must, please
Fall on your knees.

Anna Bunsen de Bary

February 17th

Walking with Grief

Do not hurry as you walk with grief
It does not help the journey.
Walk slowly, pausing often
Do not hurry as you walk with grief.
Be not disturbed if memories come unbidden.
Swiftly forgive: and let Christ speak for you unspoken words.
Unfinished conversation will be resolved in him.
Be not disturbed.
Be gentle with the one who walks with grief.
If it is you, be gentle with yourself.
Swiftly forgive.
Walk slowly, pausing often.
Take time.
Be gentle as you walk with grief.

Unattributed

February 18th

You have only to cut out a man's tongue and one of his gifts is gone. But on the contrary, you must destroy his very being, change him into another man and obliterate his identity before he ceases to be a loving man......He is lovable or admirable according as he has love, faith and self-control.

F.W.Robertson of Brighton

February 19th

It is difficult to explain fully why it is that our own sorrows become more bearable through the expression of another's sorrow. When we allow ourselves to be touched by the poignancy of another's griefs, our own anguish can be lessened in some unfathomable way. Self-pity is a diminishing experience if it is allowed to take hold. Real sadness on the other hand, is paradoxically enlarging. An old Chinese saying comes to mind:
'You cannot prevent the birds of sadness flying over your head. You can prevent them building nests in your hair.'

February 20th

Praise be to the God and Father of our Lord Jesus Christ, the Father of compassion and the God of all comfort, who comforts us in all our troubles, so that we can comfort those in any trouble with the comfort we ourselves have received from God. For just as the sufferings of Christ flow over into our lives, so also through Christ our comfort overflows. If we are distressed it is for your comfort and salvation; if we are comforted, it is for your comfort, which produces in you patient endurance of the same sufferings that we suffer. And our hope for you is firm, because we know that just as you share in our sufferings, so also you share in our comfort.

2 Corinthians 1: 2-7

February 21st

Lord God, we are daunted by the things which come to trouble and disturb our peace.
Help us to seek your Holy Spirit as the true Comforter - the one who comes with strength to help us overcome.
We do not pray for comfort just that we might feel more comfortable, for you often trouble those who settle in too comfortably to a life that ignores real pain in others.
We pray instead for fortitude to accept our trials and learn from them.

And we ask for grace that we may become true comforters of others who also need the strength of your Spirit.

February 22nd

When a friend broke her wrist she told me that what she was finding most frustrating was not being able to play ball with her grandchildren. She could not open and close her hand, and she realised how necessary this was to be able to play ball. We can only 'play ball' in this team game of life if we know how to use our hands to both give and to receive. If we are willing only to do one of those two things we are crippled. The heart can be like a closed fist on occasions, and we can be like a wounded bird unable to fly free if we do not exercise the power of giving and receiving. There is an interdependence and a balance in God's order of things. We need not only to forgive but to accept forgiveness. We need not only to open our hearts and minds in our search for knowledge and truth, but to reject what we perceive to be falsehood and superficiality. We have to seek and find; to know and then to accept the unknowing. Most of all, we have not only to receive love, but also to be willing to give love - which sometimes may mean unconditional love. The standards of Christ are very high in this. He asks us to give our love as he did without bounds. We must open those clenched fists so that we both give and receive. Every clenched fist can become again an open palm.

February 23rd

AN AFRICAN MEDITATION

When a gift is given, our reaction is to close the hand, to keep the gift so that it may not slip away. But just as surely as God gives, he comes to claim the physical things; a parent, a marriage partner, our work, our physical health, at last life itself. And when the hand is closed, God's taking back hurts us. But keep the hand open. For as surely as God comes to take back that which he has given, it is only so that he might give us a greater gift.

February 24th

A book which I return to many times, is the classic 'Kristin Lavransdatter' by the Nobel prizewinner Sigrid Undset, about life in 14th century Norway. Simon Darre, one of the characters felt the great burden he owed to another of the main characters, his brother-in-law Erland. He owed him his very life. Now the Lord's Prayer in Norwegian is as we say it in Scotland, 'Forgive us our *debts* as we forgive our *debtors.*' Simon Darre wished that the Lord had also taught us to pray, 'Forgive us our *creditors.*' He found no difficulty in forgiving his debtors, but he found it very hard to forgive Erland for laying such a burden of debt on his shoulders.

C.S. Lewis once said of an acquaintance, 'She's the sort of woman who lives for others. You can always tell the others by their hunted expression.'

February 25th

Moses Maimonides was an Israeli who lived in the 12th century. He said there were eight degrees in giving for charity, each one higher than the other.

He who gives grudgingly, reluctantly, or with regret.
He who gives less than he should, but gives graciously.
He who gives what he should, but only after he is asked.
He who gives before he is asked.
He who gives without knowing to whom he gives, although the recipient knows the identity of the donor.
He who gives without making his identity known.
He who gives without knowing to whom he gives, and the recipient not knowing from whom he receives.
He who helps a fellowman to support himself by a gift, or a loan, or by finding employment for him, thus helping him to become self-supporting.

February 26th

New York Beggar's Placard: 'Sorry! I don't accept coins. I have holes in my pockets.'

February 27th

One man gives freely, yet gains even more;
another withholds unduly, but comes to poverty.
A generous man will prosper;
he who refreshes others will himself be refreshed.
People curse the man who hoards grain,
but blessing crowns him who is willing to sell.
He who seeks good, finds goodwill,
but evil comes to him who searches for it.
Whoever trusts in his riches will fall
but the righteous will thrive like a green leaf.
The fruit of the righteous is a tree of life,
and he who wins souls is wise.

Proverbs 11: 24 -28 & 30

February 28th

Lord,
Fill us we pray with your light and life
That we may show forth your wondrous glory.
Grant that your love may so fill our lives
That we may count nothing too small to do for you
Nothing too much to give
And nothing too hard to bear.

Ignatius Loyola

February 29th

Working out the exact calendar has always been a major problem for all humankind. All calendars have had to take into account the sun, moon and stars, and of course our own is ecclesiastically based as well. A French Republican calendar was worked out and used between 1792 and 1806 as the revolutionaries wanted to abandon all connections with ecclesiastical matters, so they made a calendar with twelve months of 30 days each and five days which were festivals. They still had to add an extra festival every Leap Year to make up the full 365¼days which almost exactly form a year. That is not quite an exact figure but the discrepancy is made less by using just some of the centuries as Leap Years. An ordinary Leap Year is divisible by 4 but a century Leap year has to be divisible by 400. So the year 2000 was a Leap Year, the first century to be so since 1600.

MARCH

daffodils
That come before the swallow dares, and take
The winds of March with beauty;

Shakespeare

March 1st

Like a lot of seventeenth century poets, Robert Herrick was a clergyman, educated at Cambridge. Though he mixed with the intellectuals of his time much of his poetry had a folksy quality and some thought it rather childish. Yet as long as fifty years after his death, the rural parishioners of Dean Prior in Devonshire where he had his vicarage, were heard quoting his poetry. The following is an extract of his thanksgiving to God for his home.

Lord, thou hast given me a cell
  wherein to dwell;
A little house, whose humble roof
  is weather proof;
Under the spars of which I lie
  both soft and dry;
Where thou my chamber for to ward
  hast set a guard
Of harmless thoughts, to watch and keep
  me, while I sleep.

Some brittle sticks of thorn or briar
  make me a fire,
Close by whose living coal I sit
  and glow like it.
Lord, I confess too, when I dine,
  the pulse is thine.
And all those other bits that be
  there placed by thee.
The worts, the purslain and the mess
  of watercress

Which of thy kindness thou hast sent;
  and my content
Makes those and my beloved beet,
  to be more sweet.

Thou mak'st my teeming hen to lay
her egg each day;
Besides my healthful ewes to bear
me twins each year:
The while the conduits of my kine
run cream (for wine)
All these and better thou dost send
me, to this end,
That I should render for my part,
a thankful heart;
Which, fired with incense I resign,
as wholly thine;
But the acceptance, that must be,
my Christ by thee.

March 2nd

It is extraordinary how many poets and writers have had to leave their native land to write poetically about it - notably perhaps the Irish. They are very nostalgic about their roots, but as one of them said perceptively, 'I'd rather be homesick than home.'

March 3rd

When the journalist Jeffrey Barnard was in St Bernard's Hospital, Hanwell, yet once again the victim of his own maltreatment of his body, he fantasised about writing his own obituary, saying as he usually did to himself, that he would make sure tomorrow would be different. This is the wry obituary he wrote for himself at that time: "Thinking that geographical changes would solve his problems, he moved to various 'dream' cottages in the country. Unfortunately he was always there too. He leaves two unwritten books and a circle of detached acquaintances."

To every man there openeth
A way and a way and a way.
And the high soul climbs the high way
And the low soul gropes the low
And in between on the misty flats
The rest drift to and fro.
But to every man there openeth
A highway and a low
And every man decideth
The way his soul should go.

John Oxenham

March 4th

Jeffrey Barnard always said it would be just his luck to depart from this life on the same day as the Queen Mother, when his going would be unnoticed. He didn't quite achieve that, but he died in the same week as Princess Diana, Mother Theresa and George Solti, the famous conductor.

Yet there were many who noted his going. There were eulogies for all of them, but none to compare with that in Pilgrim's Progress for Mr. Valiant - Heart. 'He passed over - and the trumpets sounded for him on the other side.'

March 5th

Mother Theresa once said to Malcolm Muggeridge that she had come more and more to realise that being unwanted is the worst disease that any human being can experience. She said that nowadays we had found medicine for leprosy, so lepers could be cured. There's medicine for tuberculosis, so consumptives could be cured. But as for being unwanted - except when there are willing hands to serve and a loving heart to love - she said she didn't think the disease of being unwanted could ever be cured.

March 6th

How lovely is your dwelling place,
O Lord Almighty!

Even the sparrow has found a home,
and the swallow a nest for herself,
where she may have her young -
a place near your altar.
O Lord Almighty, my King and my God.
Blessed are those who dwell in your house;
they are ever praising you.

Better is one day in your courts
than a thousand elsewhere;
I would rather be a doorkeeper in the house of my God
than dwell in the tents of the wicked.
For the Lord God is a sun and a shield;
the Lord bestows favour and honour;
no good thing does he withhold
from those whose walk is blameless.

O Lord God Almighty,
blessed is the man who trusts in you.

Psalm 84: verses 1, 3-4, & 10-12

March 7th

Watch, dear Lord, with those who watch or weep tonight.
And give your angels charge over those who sleep.
Tend your sick ones, O Lord Christ,
Rest your weary ones
Bless your dying ones,
Soothe your suffering ones,
Pity your afflicted ones,
Shield your joyous ones
And all for your Love's sake   Amen

St. Augustine

March 8th

A wonderful very old lady of my acquaintance was being given her annual MOT test by her physician to see how her mind and body were functioning in her rapidly declining years. She had always a most sharp sense of humour and when she was asked the standard question in those tests, 'Can you tell me the name of the present Prime Minister?' she rapidly replied, 'Not on my visiting list!' It was never discovered if she realised she had forgotten, but had no intention of revealing this, or if she was as usual, gently teasing. But it was evident too what her priorities were in her old age. Prime Ministers come and go, but what is vitally important to each one of us is to recognise those who remain faithful enough to us to be on our visiting list, whether in person, by a letter or a telephone call, and who will succour us in our need, whatever that need may be.

March 9th

He was a friend to man and lived in a house by the side of the road.

Homer

A highland crofter was asked if he made a good living from his small-holding and he replied, 'Only just!' His questioner then said he could not understand why he was not taking the opportunity to acquire the neighbouring croft to expand his profits. 'Och no,' he said. 'If I did that I wouldn't have a neighbour.'

March 10th

Lord Mackay of Clashfern said once that he didn't think the last words of any human being would be, 'I wish I'd spent more time at the office.' Nowadays there are large parts of our homes where massive space is taken up by computers, televisions, answerphones, mobile phones, digital this and laser that - all kinds of modern technology. Our homes are in fact becoming more and more like our offices. We need jealously to guard the time we have available for human beings, with a view to devoting to them what has come to be called 'Quality time.' For despite all our modern aids - washing machines, fast foods, micro-wave ovens - we have not more but less time for just giving ourselves to each other in *companionship.*

> Mechanic soul, you must not only do
> With Martha, but with Mary too.
> Happy is the house where those fair sisters vary;
> But most, where Martha's reconciled with Mary.
>
> *Francis Quarles*

March 11th

A writer J.G. Ballard has said that on his travels he became very addicted to the Yellow Pages in the telephone directory. He was fascinated to discover in Los Angeles that there were listed far more psychiatrists than plumbers, and far more marriage counsellors than electricians.

There is surely some kind of message for us all in that interesting comment.

March 12th

It has become desirable to introduce into many places of work a writer in residence so that those who who are bogged down with technical matters have an opportunity to relate to the creative side of life - spirit and soul. The experiment has lately been carried also into hospitals and hospices, where patients are encouraged to release their feelings and imagination in creative writing. One member of the nursing staff when asked about encouraging this in her ward, said that she could not really understand the need for it, unless it was to help the patients with the writing of their wills!

March 13th

For God, who said, 'Let light shine out of darkness,' made his light shine in our hearts to give us the light of the knowledge of the glory of God in the face of Christ.
But we have this treasure in jars of clay to show that this all-surpassing power is from God and not from us.
We are hard-pressed on every side, but not crushed; perplexed, but not in despair; persecuted, but not abandoned; struck down, but not destroyed.
We always carry around in our body the death of Jesus, so that the life of Jesus may also be revealed in our body.

2 Corinthians 4: 6-10

March 14th

Take this moment, sign and space
Take my friends around;
here among us make a place
where your love is found.

Take the time to call my name
Take the time to mend
who I am and what I've been
all I've failed to tend.

Take the tiredness of my days
Take my past regrets
letting your forgiveness touch
all I can't forget.

Take the little child in me
scared of growing old;
help me here to find my worth
made in Christ's own mould.

Take my talents, take my skills
take what's yet to be;
let my life be yours and yet
let it still be me.

John Bell and Graham Maule

March 15th

I came on a very curious bit of information the other day, which baffled me on two counts.

First, I didn't understand how anyone had managed to work it out about two centuries before the computer age. Secondly, I wondered about the purpose of what seemed to me a sterile fact, which stated that there is only one verse in the Authorised version of the Bible which uses every letter of our alphabet except J. The verse is Ezra 7: 21.

I remember a young minister once saying to me after he had completed his theology degree that he had been taught amongst other things how many 'ands' and 'buts' there were in the Acts of the Apostles, but no-one had ever taught him how to make a pastoral visit to the old and lonely widow imprisoned in her top tenement flat. We can so easily get our priorities all topsy - turvy. John Betjeman used some apt words about the old lady in Felixstowe who 'put her shilling in the meter and made her loneliness completer.'

March 16th

If with pleasure you are viewing
any work a man is doing,
If you like him and you trust him,
tell him now.
Don't withhold your approbation,
till the person makes oration
And he lies with snowy lilies on his brow.
For no matter how you shout it,
he won't know a thing about it,
For he cannot read his tombstone when he's dead.

Or as the song 'The Living Years' has it, 'Say it now! And say it clear!' Isn't it strange that we most often refer to 'loved ones' after they have departed this life?

March 17th

This day is not only St. Patrick's Day, but also that on which Joseph of Arimathea is remembered. He was a rich Jew who believed in Christ, but was afraid to confess his belief. After the Crucifixion, he begged for the body of Christ and deposited it in his own garden tomb.

That we know from the Gospel stories, but legends have grown up that he was imprisoned thereafter for 12 years and was kept alive by the Holy Grail, the cup used for the wine at the last supper. The legend goes that he brought the Grail to Glastonbury, along with the sword that pierced Christ. The legends and romance continued to expand, including the adventures of the knights of the Round Table. But no part of the legend compares in value with the wonderful true story of the Crucifixion and Resurrection, of which Joseph of Arimathea was a part.

> Opinion is a flitting thing
> But Truth outlasts the sun
> If then we cannot own them both
> Possess the older one.

Emily Dickinson

March 18th

> Truth forever on the scaffold
> Wrong forever on the throne,
> Yet that scaffold rules the future
> And behind the dim unknown
> Standeth God within the shadows
> Keeping watch above his own.

James Russell Lowell

March 19th

Here is an anonymous Civil Servant's Prayer. I don't wonder at the need for anonymity.

> O Lord, who sees all things below
> Grant that your servants may go slow
> That they may struggle to comply
> With regulations till they die.
>
> Teach us, O Lord, to reverence
> Committees more than common-sense;
> To train our minds to make no plan
> And pass the baby when we can.
>
> So when the tempter seems to give
> Us feelings of initiative,
> Or when alone we go too far,
> Chastise us with a circular.
>
> Mid war and tumult, fire and storms,
> Give strength, O Lord, to deal out forms
> Thus may your servants ever keep
> Intact the flock of perfect sheep.

March 20th

So then, just as you received Christ Jesus as Lord, continue to live in him, rooted and built up in him, strengthened in the faith as you were taught, and overflowing with thankfulness.
See to it that no-one takes you captive through hollow and deceptive philosophy, which depends on human tradition and the basic principles of this world rather than on Christ.

Colossians 2: 6 -7

March 21st

You are my Life.
If you but turn away, my life's a thousand deaths.
You are my Way.
Without you, Lord, I travel not, but stray.
My Light you are.
Without your glorious sight,
my eyes are darkened with perpetual night.
My God, you are my Way, my Life, my Light.
You are my Way.
I wander if you fly.
You are my Light.
If hid, how blind am I.
You are my Life.
If you withdraw, I die.
Disclose your sunbeams.
Close your wings, and stay.
See how I'm blind, and dead and stray.
O Lord, you are my Light, my Life, my Way.

Francis Quarles

March 22nd

The Proper Study

Seated before her window, Mrs. Jones
Described the passers-by in ringing tones
'Look,' she would say, 'The girl at Number Three
Has brought her latest boy-friend home to tea;
And see, the woman in the upstairs flat
Has bought herself another summer hat.'
Her daughter, Daphne, filled with deep disgust
Expostulated, 'Mother, really must
You pry upon the neighbours? Don't you know
Gossip is idle, empty-minded, low?'

And Mrs. Jones would murmur, 'Fancy, dear!
There's Mr. Thompson going for his beer.'

Daphne, an earnest girl of twenty-three
Read Sociology for her degree
And every Saturday she would repair
Armed with her latest questionnaire,
To knock on doors, demanding, 'Are you wed?
Have you a child? A car? A double bed?'
Poor Mrs. Jones would remonstrate each week,
'Daphne, I wonder how you have the cheek!
And then *you* call me nosy!' Daphne sighed.
'Oh, will you never understand?' she cried,
Mere curiosity is one thing, Mother!
Social analysis is quite another!'

W.S.Slater

March 23rd

The American Indians have a saying, 'Before you judge a person, walk in his moccasins for three moons.'
That is maybe what empathy is all about.

March 24th

A fanatic is someone who can't change his mind, and who refuses to change the subject.

March 25th

You cannot hope to bribe or twist
Thank God! the British journalist.
But, seeing what the man will do
Unbribed, there's no occasion to.

Humbert Wolfe

March 26th

True hospitality means making folk feel at home, when you really wish they were.

March 27th

In the last days there will be scoffers who will follow their own ungodly desires. These are the men who divide you, who follow mere natural instincts and do not have the Spirit. But you, dear friends, hold yourself up in your most holy faith and pray in the

Holy Spirit. To him who is able to keep you from falling and to present you before his glorious presence without fault and with great joy - to the only God our Saviour be glory, majesty, power and authority, through Jesus Christ our Lord, before all ages, now and for evermore. Amen.

Jude: 18-20 & 24-25

March 28th

Give me, O Lord, a steadfast heart
which no unworthy affection may drag downwards
Give me an unconquered heart
which no tribulation can wear out
Give me an upright heart
which no unworthy purpose may tempt aside
Bestow on me also, O Lord my God
understanding to know you
diligence to seek you
wisdom to find you
And a faithfulness that may finally embrace you
through Jesus Christ our Lord

Thomas Aquinas

March 29th

Henry Ford, famous for his Model T cars, had a long and happy marriage. When he was once asked the secret, he said, 'It's the same formula I use for cars - just stick to one model!'

March 30th

To wash dirty linen in public, with great display
Makes dirty linen dirtier every day.

March 31st

Someone discussing the Pilgrim Fathers and their hardships, said that you never seemed to hear much about the Pilgrim Mothers. But the fact of the matter is that they put up with exactly the same hardships, and what is more, they had to put up with the Pilgrim Fathers as well!

JUST LIKE A MAN

He sat at the dinner table
With a discontented frown,
The potatoes and steak were underdone
And the bread was baked too brown;
The pie was too sour and the pudding too sweet
And the roast was much too fat;
The soup was greasy too and salt,
'Twas hardly fit for the cat.

'I wish you could eat the bread and pie
I've seen my mother make,
They are something like, and 'twould do you good
Just to look at a loaf of her cake.'
Said the smiling wife, 'I'll improve with age -
Just now I'm but a beginner;
But your mother has come to visit us,
And today *she* cooked the dinner.'

Anonymous

'AWAITING THE DAWN'

Meditations as we approach Easter

Approaching Easter (1)

The other day I came on some unsophisicated snapshots I had taken on my one and only trip to the Holy Land, quite a number of years back. I was not surprised to find that very few of those photos were of buildings, for most of my memories of what I call 'moments of illumination' are associated with the out-of-door places. I have always been greatly affected by what is commonly called 'spirit of place' - those numinous sites where one is conscious of an atmosphere creating an awe which is generally associated with religion and God. I don't know why it happens, or if it only happens when one already knows something of the history of a place and something about those who once lived there. I have certainly felt the spirit of place in Lindisfarne, Iona, Durham where Bede and Cuthbert walked, and also strangely at Delphi in Greece.

I wish I could return to Galilee and its environs, for I was particularly aware of what it could have been like when Christ walked there nearly 2000 years ago.

One of my snapshots has written on it 'Storm rising on Galilee.' I, and another free spirit in our holiday group, had broken free one afternoon and taken a boat from Tiberias to go to climb the Golan Heights which had been so much in the news. The lake was beautiful and peaceful, but before we reached the shore, the captain's voice came over the loud hailer, saying that all passengers would be given instructions on landing about how to return later round the lake by bus. A storm was brewing, and all boats would be staying in the shelter of the fishing ports. We could not believe it, as the lake still looked so calm and peaceful. But my picture was taken minutes later, and we never saw another ship on the lake of Galilee that afternoon.

This freshwater lake which is about 13 miles long and 7 miles wide is a focal point in the life of Jesus. It is surrounded by hills, and funnelling down through them races the wind which can whip up the water very suddenly into a fury.

So there was this moment of illumination when my friend and myself realised the full significance of the calming presence of Christ with his disciples on a storm-tossed lake. Jesus was in the boat but this did not stop difficulties arising. But when trouble came, his presence made all the difference - not only to the situation, but to the awe and wonder and faith of those who were with him.

We should cherish the ecstatic, glowing experiences, but we must also cherish the validity of God's presence when we feel afraid. As we approach the journey of Christ to Calvary from this area which was so familiar to him, we may start with his familiar words on the Sea of Galilee which are for us also, 'Why are you so afraid? Do you still have no faith?' Lent and Easter are good times to re-evaluate our faith, as we travel the journey with Christ from Galilee to his death and resurrection in Jerusalem.

Immortal love, forever full,
Forever flowing free,
Forever shared, forever whole
A never ebbing sea!
We may not climb the heavenly steeps
To bring the Lord Christ down.
In vain we search the lowest deeps,
For him no depths can drown.
But warm, sweet, tender, even yet
A present help is he;
And faith has still its Olivet
And love its Galilee.

John Greenleaf Whittier

Approaching Easter (2)

After we left the shores of Galilee and climbed up the Golan Heights, I took another snapshot of the bounty of colourful wild flowers amongst which we stood to look at the now storm-tossed lake. Christ said in the Sermon on the Mount that even Solomon in all his glory was not equal to this beauty. We were reminded of the Beatitudes, or the Blessed Attitudes as someone has aptly described them. But our gentle thoughts were interrupted as we climbed on upwards towards the plateau. Approaching was a crocodile of school children and their two teachers, but at the front and back of the line was a forbidding looking soldier with weapons ready in case of trouble. I remembered many outdoor nature walks with my pupils on the hills behind my Scottish rural school, and I was troubled by the contrast. Here at Galilee the hopes and fears of all the years were indeed met for me at that moment.

slave and freeman, rich and poor, old and young were without exception included in the 'whosoever' promised eternal life through his love and sacrifice. I was still to travel to Jerusalem and still to have to bend low to enter in the Church of the Nativity in Bethlehem what was probably the site of the cave where this Christ was born. But I had already experienced something of the awe of the shepherds who had come down from their nightshift carefully tending their sheep to kneel before their Messiah. I wanted to meet him again at Gethsemane.

Christ who knows all his sheep
  Will all in safety keep;
He will not lose his blood
  Nor intercession:
Nor we the purchased good
  Of his dear passion.

Lord Jesus, take my spirit
  I trust thy love and merit:
Take home this wandering sheep
  For thou hast sought it:
This soul in safety keep
  For thou hast bought it.

Richard Baxter

Approaching Easter (5)

I suppose the Garden of Gethsemane, on the Mount of Olives, is for pilgrims, one of the most treasured sites in the Holy Land. I never think of it now without thinking of the aftermath of the Dunblane Massacre when those very young pupils and their teacher were gunned down just a short while before Easter. I remember the numbness with which I pondered the news. I had many, many questions to ask of God, as I have often had to do personally when confronting personal griefs. My thoughts were turned to Gethsemane where Christ himself felt God had forsaken him. If the Lord Christ himself could question, why could not I? At least in our questioning we are engaging with God, and finding paradoxically him and Christ in the very doubts we are expressing.

After Dunblane a Scot who had just returned from Gethsemane told us that at the entrance to one of the churches in Gethsemane were the words,' Please, no questions within the church.'

The holy places in Palestine suffer from the milling crowds, the tourist buses, the guides' voices, explaining, explaining, explaining. It is good to make a space at Gethsemane where we lay our questions aside and like the man in R.S. Thomas's poem 'In Church', test our faith on emptiness and nail our questions one by one 'to the untenanted cross.' Our questioning can seem paltry when we are faced with Christ crucified. For Christ's agony in Gethsemane among the gnarled, twisted old olive trees which we can still see today, is only acceptable when we go forward from there to the Cross and then the resurrection. There is a strange paradox that one needs to experience the darkness in order to experience the enlightenment.

> O Joy that seekest me through pain,
> I cannot close my heart to thee:
> I trace the rainbow through the rain,
> And feel the promise is not vain,
> That morn shall tearless be.
>
> O Cross that liftest up my head,
> I dare not ask to fly from thee:
> I lay in dust life's glory dead,
> And from the ground there blossoms red
> Life that shall endless be.

George Matheson

Approaching Easter (6)

It was a very hot day in Jerusalem when we were making the journey which is traditionally regarded as the way of the cross. We were invited to meditate on some of the incidents in the progress of Jesus from his trial before Pilate to the laying of his body in the tomb. We were to walk from Pilate's house to Calvary. The old streets were crowded and tiring and some of us became extremely thirsty. We asked our leader about the possibilities of quenching our thirst and he arranged for a stop where we had the most delicious fresh orange juice, squeezed to order and chilled. I realised how hard it would have been to continue that walk if my thirst, which had been stronger than any thirst I had ever experienced, had not been dealt with in the searing heat.

I have often thought since of that moment when Christ said on the cross, 'I thirst.' It was the day of Crucifixion, with all the heat, the noise, the dust that we experienced in the same area. Seven times Jesus spoke on the cross, but this was the only time he spoke of his own suffering and human need. One of the soldiers went forward to moisten his lips. I never cease to be moved by the revelation here of the humanity of Christ and I am humbled to think that a soldier could be one of the human beings around the cross to realise his needs.

As I think of Christ hanging between the two thieves, one on his left and one on his right, one repentant and one rebellious, I am drawn to the earlier words of the sons of Zebedee, James and John, who wanted Christ to allow them the privilege when he came into his glory of sitting one on his left and one on his right. How ironic now when they looked at those on his left and right. They would remember with pain Christ's answer to them, 'You do not know what you are asking. Can you drink the cup I must drink of?'

We must stand at the cross again ourselves and realise what it meant for Christ that first Good Friday. And though we do not fully understand it, accept that this death, so many generations before we were born, was for us. His own words are 'For God so loved the world that he gave his only begotten Son, that whosoever believes on him, should not perish but have everlasting life.'

> This is the night of tears, the three days' space,
> Sorrow abiding of the eventide
> Until the day break with the risen Christ,
> And hearts that sorrowed shall be satisfied.
>
> So may our hearts have pity on thee, Lord,
> That they may sharers of thy glory be:
> Heavy with weeping may the three days pass.
> To win the laughter of thine Easter day.
>
> *Peter Abelard*

Approaching Easter (7)

The emotions of Christ's followers on the day after his crucifixion must have been full of mourning and emptiness and in cases like Peter, overwhelmed with remorse. There were some like Joseph of Arimathea who had cared for the body of Jesus.

The women would have been on this Jewish Sabbath day probably preparing the spices ready for their early morning visit to the garden tomb. But there must have been many in Jerusalem who had already dismissed the scene from their minds. In our secular society, it is salutary on this day before resurrection day to ponder this poem of Studdert Kennedy's, and to ask ourselves how much we really care. Or have we tended to be just indifferent?

Indifference

When Jesus came to Golgotha they hanged him on a tree,
They drave great nails through hands and feet, and made a
 Calvary,
They crowned him with a crown of thorns, red were his wounds
 and deep,
For those were crude and cruel days, and human flesh was cheap.

When Jesus came to Birmingham, they simply passed him by,
They never hurt a hair of him, they only let him die;
For men had grown more tender, and they would not give him
 pain,
They only passed down the street, and left him in the rain.

Still Jesus cried, 'Forgive them, for they know not what they do,'
And still it rained the winter rain that drenched him through and
 through;
The crowds went home and left the streets without a soul to see,
And Jesus crouched against a wall and cried for Calvary.

EASTER DAY

Christ is risen! Alleluia

When I was in Jerusalem, I went back alone to the garden tomb which, although it may not be the exact place which Joseph of Arimathea gave for Christ's body, is typical of the garden burial places used in Christ's day. I found several moments of illumination there. I was struck by the fact that to enter the tomb, you had to bow down and you had to enter one at a time.

As I walked alone later through the peaceful and beautiful garden surrounding the burial place, it was easy to enter into the feelings of Mary as she walked there, weeping, thinking her Lord's body was stolen.

Those of us who have spent time teaching young children to cope with the vagaries of the English language can well accept the classic story of the youngster trying to read the graffiti on a wall which read 'God is nowhere.' He pointed to it and said to his mother, 'Why has somebody written, "God is NOW HERE"?'

Mary thought she had lost her Lord and her God. She wanted to find him, and pleaded with the one she thought to be the gardener, to show her where she might find him. She thought that he was nowhere around anymore. But in fact he was not nowhere but NOW HERE, here in the very garden where she was grieving his loss. And he found her, as he found the other followers, in the hours and days which followed. We may feel we are still seeking him in our lives. But if with all our hearts we truly seek him, we shall ever surely find him, for he has been seeking us before ever we knew it.

Halts by me that footfall:
Is my gloom, after all,
Shade of his hand, outstretched caressingly?
'Ah, fondest, blindest, weakest,
I am he whom thou seekest!
Thou dravest love from thee, who dravest me.'

Francis Thompson

Let us rejoice in the words of the wonderful resurrection hymn now often sung triumphantly to Handel's Chorus from Judas Maccabæus.

Lo! Jesus meets us, risen from the tomb;
Lovingly he greets us, scatters fear and gloom;
Let the Church with gladness, hymns of triumph sing
For her Lord now liveth, death hath lost its sting.

Thine be the glory, risen, conquering Son,
Endless is the victory, thou o'er death hast won.

No more we doubt thee, glorious Prince of Life;
Life is naught without thee; aid us in our strife;
Make us more than conquerors, through thy deathless love;
Bring us safe through Jordan to thy home above.

Thine be the glory, risen, conquerering Son,
Endless is the victory, thou o'er death hast won.

Edmond Budry translated by *R. B. Hoyle*

Here is an Easter prayer written by my own minister, Malcolm Ramsay.

God of the Resurrection,
    I praise you
        for all the wonderful ways
    in which I see new life bursting out
        in your world;
    in green shoots, and in nesting birds;
    in the bright enthusiasms of young children;
    in the signs of rekindled hope within your church.
But above all, I praise you
    for raising your Son Jesus Christ
        from the dead
on that first Easter Day.

APRIL

'..... relish each one of the days of April, the month that tastes of childhood
George MacKay Brown

April 1st

Christopher Smart was another Cambridge fellow who wrote poetry. Some of his publications were encouraged by Dr. Samuel Johnson, but like many poets today, he found it hard to make a living and spent some time in prison for debt. He died before he was fifty in 1771 after being declared insane. His poems were very long and in some cases extraordinary, not least in the one I now quote where he on several occasions mentions electricity, as 'For by stroking of him I have found out electricity.'

From Jubilate Agno

For I will consider my cat Jeffery.
For he is the servant of the living God, duly and daily serving him.
For at the first glance of the glory of God in the east he worships in his way,
For this is done by wreathing his body seven times round with elegant quickness;
For then he leaps up to catch the musk, which is the blessing of God upon his prayer.
For he rolls upon prank to work it in.
For having done duty and received blessing he begins to consider himself.
For this he performs in ten degrees.
For first he looks at his forepaws to see that they are clean.
For secondly he kicks up behind to clear away there.
For thirdly he works it upon stretch with forepaws extended.
For fourthly he sharpens his paws by wood.
For fifthly he washes himself.
For sixthly he rolls upon wash.
For seventhly he fleas himself, that he may not be interrupted upon the beat.
For eighthly he rubs himself against a post
For ninthly he looks up for his instructions.
For tenthly he goes in quest of food.
For having considered God and himself he will consider his neighbour.

For if he meets another cat he will kiss her in kindness.
For when he takes his prey he plays with it to give it chance.
For one mouse in seven escapes by his dallying.
For he keeps the Lord's watch in the night against the adversary.
For he counteracts the powers of darkness by his electrical skin and glaring eyes.
For he counteracts the Devil who is death, by brisking about the life.
For in his morning orisons he loves the sun and the sun loves him.

....

For he purrs in thankfulness when God tells him that he is a good cat
For he is an instrument for the children to learn benevolence upon...

....

For he knows that God is his Saviour
For there is nothing sweeter than his peace when he is at rest.

April 2nd

Cats are rather delicate creatures and they are subject to a good many different ailments, but I have never met one that suffered from insomnia.

Joseph Wood Ktutch

April 3rd

A Cat's Conscience

A dog will often steal a bone,
But conscience lets him not alone,
And by his tail his guilt is known.

But cats consider theft a game,
And howsoever you may blame,
Refuse the slightest sign of shame.

When food mysteriously goes,
The chances are that Pussy knows
More than she leads you to suppose.

And hence there is no need for you,
If Puss declines a meal or two,
To feel her pulse or make ado.

Anon

April 4th

One of the philosophers tells the story of a child watching a sculptor studying a large block of granite.

'What are you looking for?' said the child.

The sculptor told him to wait and see. Later the child returned to find that the sculptor had almost finished carving a beautiful horse.

The child stared in amazement and then asked wonderingly, 'How did you know that it was in there?'

God can give us the perception to see the potential in whatever or whomsoever we encounter. But we don't always use that potential.

Paul Theroux once said that the first time he ever saw the Queen, it only served to remind him that he needed to buy some stamps.

April 5th

The Bible contains much that is relevant today, like Noah taking 40 days to find a place to park.

Curtis D. MacDougall

April 6th

The Spirit of the Lord will rest on him-
the Spirit of wisdom and of understanding,
the Spirit of counsel and of power,
the Spirit of knowledge and the fear of the Lord -

The wolf will live with the lamb,
the leopard will lie down with the goat,
the calf and the lion and the yearling together;
and a little child shall lead them.
The cow will feed with the bear,
their young will lie down together,
and the lion will eat straw like the ox.

The infant will play near the hole of the cobra,
and the young child put his hand into the viper's nest.
They will neither harm nor destroy on all my holy
mountain,
for the earth will be full of the knowledge of the Lord
as the waters cover the sea.

Isaiah 11: 2 & 6-9

April 7th

Lord God, our Creator, we know you have a care for all your creation, for Christ himself told us that not even a sparrow falls to the ground but what you know about it. We cannot comprehend the breadth and depth of such care and compassion. But we accept that this knowledge was given to us by your Son who was himself called the Lamb of God, who came to redeem the world and to take away the sins of the world. Help us in humility to follow him and his example.

April 8th

The Donkey

When fishes flew and forests walked
  And figs grew upon thorn,
Some moment when the moon was blood
  Then surely I was born.

With monstrous head and sickening cry
  And ears like errant wings
The devil's walking parody
  On all four-footed things.

The tattered outlaw of the earth
  Of ancient crooked will;
Starve, scourge, deride me: I am dumb,
  I keep my secret still.

Fools! For I also had my hour;
  One far fierce hour and sweet:
There was a shout about my ears,
  And palms before my feet.

G.K. Chesterton

April 9th

Love is an act of endless forgiveness: a look that becomes a habit.

Peter Ustinov

April 10th

Money won't buy happiness. But it will pay the salaries of a large research staff to study the problem.

Bill Vaughan

April 11th

The past is history
The future mystery
But today's a gift
That's why it's called the present.

Unattributed

April 12th

APRIL EVENING

All in the April evening
April airs were abroad;
The sheep with their little lambs
Passed me by on the road.
The sheep with their little lambs
Passed me by on the road
All in the April evening
I thought on the lamb of God.

The lambs were weary and crying
With a weak, human cry,
I thought on the lamb of God
Going meekly to die.
Up in the blue, blue mountains
Dewy pastures are sweet,
Rest for the little bodies,
Rest for the little feet.

But for the Lamb, the Lamb of God,
Up on the hilltop green,
Only a cross, a cross of shame,
Two stark crosses between.
All in the April evening,
April airs were abroad;
I saw the sheep with their lambs,
And thought on the Lamb of God.

Katherine Tynan

April 13th

Surely he hath borne our griefs and carried our sorrows: yet we did esteem him stricken, smitten of God and afflicted. But he was wounded for our transgressions, he was bruised for our iniquities: the chastisement of our peace was upon him; and with his stripes we are healed.

All we like sheep have gone astray; we have turned every one to his own way; and the Lord hath laid on him the iniquity of us all. He was oppressed, and he was afflicted, yet he opened not his mouth: he was brought as a lamb to the slaughter, and as a sheep before her shearers is dumb, so he openeth not his mouth.

....

He was numbered with the transgressors; and he bare the sins of many, and made intercession for the transgressors.

Isaiah 53:4-7 & 12

April 14th

An Indian Prayer

O Tree of Calvary
send your roots deep down
into my heart.
Gather together the soil of my heart,
the sands of my fickleness,
the stones of my stubbornness,
the mud of my desires,
bind them all together,
O Tree of Calvary.
Interlace them with your strong roots,
entwine them with the network
of your love.

Chandran Devanesen

April 15th

The Curé d'Ars was a nineteenth century French priest known for his pastoral care. Jean Louis Chaffington was an old man who spent most of his days at the back of his church. When the priest asked him what he did there all day, he answered, 'I look at Him. He looks at me.'
The Curé d'Ars said that is what it means to be drawn into silent prayer.

April 16th

An elderly man retired to the area where I live and he told a true similar story to that of the Curé d'Ars. He used to live opposite a little church and at noon each day he watched Jim, an old man, enter the church and remain within it for a period. One day he did not come, and after finding out that he had gone into hospital, my elderly acquaintance decided to visit him.

He said to Jim, 'I used to watch you go into the church opposite where I live at noon everyday. Why did you do that?'

'I don't really have much idea about prayer. So I decided to go into the church and just sit quietly and say, "Hallo Jesus. This is Jim here."'

'And what do you do now that you can't go into the church?'

'Well, it's just the same, really. At noon I lie on my bed and think what it would be like to be in the church. But it's different too. Because it's "Hallo, Jim. This is Jesus here."'

April 17th

When I am away from home, I like to go into an empty open church and sit quietly and think of all those who worshipped there in past years. It gives me a strange sense of the communion of saints when I think of my prayers and petitions being mingled with those of generations past and generations to come. Sadly, because of the society we now live in, with its vandalism and disregard for consecrated places, it is becoming increasingly difficult to find churches open outwith hours of worship.

'There can be no surer sign of decay in a country than to see the rites of religion held in contempt.'

Niccolo Machiavelli (1469 - 1527)

April 18th

Child to Mother, after saying prayers: Does God always remember to leave his answer phone switched on?

April 19th

Socrates lived over 400 years before Christ. This is what he wrote about the youth of his day:

'They have execrable manners; flout authority; have no respect for their elders. What kind of awful creatures will they grow up to be?'

Peter the Hermit lived over 1200 years after Christ. This is what he wrote about the youth of his day:

'The world is passing through troubled times. The young folk of today think of nothing but themselves: they have no reverence for parents or old age. They are impatient of all restraint. They talk as if they know everything, and what passes for wisdom with us is foolishness with them. As for the girls, they are foolish and immodest and unwomanly in speech and behaviour.'

The more things change, the more they remain the same.

April 20th

We who are strong ought to bear with the failings of the weak and not to please ourselves.
Each of us should please his neighbour for his good, to build him up. For even Christ did not please himself . . . .
May the God who gives endurance and encouragement give you a spirit of unity among yourselves as you follow Christ Jesus, so that with one heart and mouth you may glorify the God and Father of our Lord Jesus Christ.

Romans 15: 1-3a & 5-6

April 21st

God of Easter,

Let your reviving power
surge into the lives of the many who need you so much:
those without hope that they may hear the gospel and believe;
those without food that they may be fed;
those without fear that your grace may humble the proud and restrain the wicked;
those I know who are particularly in my thoughts and whom I lift before you now . . . .

God of the Resurrection,

Help me to rise from prayer now to live in the light of Easter and in the company of the risen Christ.
I offer this prayer in his name. Amen

Malcolm Ramsay

April 22nd

An Anglican vicar has told the story of his consultation with a young couple regarding the form of their wedding service. They requested the modern form without the word 'obey' from the wife. Later the young man returned on his own now wanting the word 'obey' included. The vicar asked what had brought about this reversal of their previous joint decision. The young man said that actually he had no strong feelings about it but the more they discussed it, the more his fiancée insisted that it must be left in.

This reminded me of the wedding which took place in a village church abroad where I was staying. The bridegroom was a rugged hardy seaman who had had a great struggle with fidelity. When told of the serious nature of the vows he would be taking, he said that all he could promise was that he would try his very best.

April 23rd

A lecturer in philosophy was asked by a student how to define conscience.

'That's a hard one,' he replied. 'All I know is that it is soluble in alcohol.'

April 24th

A cynic has said that his idea of a Christian was a man who repented on Sunday for what he did on Saturday. But he had every intention of planning to repeat the misdeeds on Monday. But as someone else has aptly said, 'Just going to church on Sunday doesn't make you a Christian any more than visiting the garage makes you a car.'

Or to put it differently, there's no use spending the week sowing your wild oats, and then just going to church on Sunday to pray for a crop failure.

April 25th

Arthur Hugh Clough is probably best known for his inspiring poem quoted by Churchill: 'Say Not The Struggle Nought Availeth.' But he could be equally challenging when he used satire, as in the following poem, of which probably only two lines are generally known and used.

The Latest Decalogue

Thou shalt have one God only; who
Would be at the expense of two?
No graven images may be
Worshipped, except the currency:
Swear not at all; for, for thy curse
Thine enemy is none the worse.
At church on Sunday to attend
Will serve to keep the world thy friend:
Honour thy parents; that is, all
From whom advancement may befall.

Thou shalt not kill; but need'st not strive
Officiously to keep alive:
Do not adultery commit;
Advantage rarely comes of it:
Thou shalt not steal; an empty feat,
When it's so lucrative to cheat:
Bear not false witness; let the lie
Have time on its own wings to fly:
Thou shalt not covet, but tradition
Approves all forms of competition.

April 26th

Bernard of Clairvaux was the founder of the Cistercian Order in the twelfth century. Many of the pieces he wrote are still of great relevance today.

'If you notice something evil in yourself, correct it; if something good, take care of it; if something beautiful, cherish it; if something sound, preserve it; if something unhealthy, heal it. Do not weary of reading the commandments of the Lord, and you will be adequately instructed by them so as to know what to avoid and what to go after.'

April 27th

Furious with rage, Nebuchadnezzar summoned Shadrach, Meshach and Abednego. So these men were brought before the king, and Nebuchadnezzar said to them, 'Is it true, Shadrach, Meschach and Abednego, that you do not serve my gods or worship the image of gold that I have set up? Now, when you hear the sound of the horn, flute, zither, lyre, harp, pipes and all kinds of music, if you are ready to fall down and worship the image I made, very good. But if you do not worship it, you will be thrown immediately into a fiery furnace. Then what god will be able to rescue you from my hand?'
Shadrach, Meschach and Abednego replied to the king, 'O Nebuchadnezzar, we do not need to defend ourselves before you in this matter. If we are thrown into the blazing furnace, the God we serve is able to save us from it, and he will rescue us from your hand, O king. But even if he does not, we want you to know, O king, that we will not serve your gods or worship the image of gold you have set up.'

Daniel 3: 13 -18

April 28th

St. Patrick's Breastplate

Against all Satan's spells and wiles,
Against false words of heresy,
Against the knowledge that defiles,
Against the heart's idolatry,
Against the wizard's evil craft,
Against the death-wound and the burning,
The choking wave and poisoned shaft,
Protect me, Lord, till your returning.

April 29th

Minister during his children's sermon: If you were told that you could have anything in the world you wanted, what would you say?
Child: Thank you!

April 30th

The mother was intent on getting her little daughter to use a knife and fork properly.

'You must never ever eat your food off your knife,' she emphasised.

The little girl made a brave effort, but became very frustrated at her lack of success.

Finally in exasperation, she cried out, 'What am I supposed to do when the fork keeps leaking?'

MANNERS

I eat my peas with honey
I've done it all my life
It makes my peas taste funny
But it keeps them on the knife.

Anon

MAY

Button to chin, till May be in;
Cast ne'er a clout, till May be out.

May 1st

I was seventeen when I first read the works of African writers and I have been fascinated by them ever since. Perhaps my favourite is The Creation by James Weldon Johnson, part of which is good to read in this burgeoning month of the year.

And God stepped out on space,
And He looked around and said:
I'm lonely -
I'll make me a world.

And far as the eye of God could see
Darkness covered everything,
Blacker than a hundred midnights
Down in a cypress swamp.

Then God smiled,
And the light broke, And the darkness rolled up on one side,
And the light stood shining on the other,
And God said, That's good!

Then God reached out and took the light in his hands,
And God rolled the light around in his hands
Until he made the sun;
And he set that sun ablazing in the heavens,
And the light that was left from making the sun
God gathered it up in a shining ball
And flung it against the darkness,
Spangling the night with the moon and the stars.
Then down between
The darkness and the light
He hurled the world;
And God said: That's good! ......

....Then God raised his arm and he waved his hand
Over the sea and over the land,
And he said, Bring forth! Bring forth!
And quicker than God could drop his hand,
Fishes and fowls

And beasts and birds
Swam the rivers and the seas,
Roamed the forests and the woods,
And split the air with their wings,
And God said, That's good!

He looked on his world
With all its living things,
And God said: I'm lonely still.

Then God sat down
On the side of a hill where he could think;
By a deep, wide river he sat down;
With his head in his hands,
God thought and thought,
Till he thought: I'll make me a man!

Up from the bed of the river
God scooped the clay;
And by the bank of the river
He kneeled him down;
And there the great God Almighty
Who lit the sun and fixed it in the sky,
Who flung the stars to the far corner of the night,
Who rounded the earth in the middle of his hand;
This great God,
Like a mammy bending over her baby,
Kneeled down in the dust
Toiling over a lump of clay
Till he shaped it in his own image;

Then into it he blew the breath of life,
And man became a living soul.
Amen. Amen.

May 2nd

A Russian astronaut who was an atheist, was in conversation with a Christian brain surgeon about very deep matters.

Astronaut: Well I've been out in space, and I've never seen God - or even an angel.

Neurosurgeon: And I've been inside the human brain many times, and I've never ever seen a single thought!

May 3rd

Professor Sir Martin Rees, Astronomer Royal once said that when he was asked how cosmology related to philosophy and religion he had a very boring answer to give - that in principle nothing had advanced very much since Newton's day. We can trace the causal chain back further than Newton was able to, but there is still a barrier beyond which we cannot go. As someone else has put it, 'The more we look, the more we see, but the mystery is never dispelled.' I believe there is something powerful and beautiful in accepting the mystery without being able to dispel it.

May 4th

I remember in 1997 when the Hale-Bopp comet was to be seen clearly in the heavens, some of us would go out evening after evening to watch it in the clear night skies. Someone who was more skilled at astronomy than we were, said he was amazed at the interest everyone was showing in this trail of dust, for that was really what it was. Yet, night after night we ignore the permanent wonders of the heavens so clearly there for us to marvel at.

Isn't it often so? - we devote more time and worship to the latest transient pleasure and miss the many-splendoured thing which God offers us in the gift of his Son.

May 5th

Isaac Newton once said that he could take his telescope and look millions of miles into space. But he had only to go to his room and engage in prayer and be nearer to God than if he employed all the telescopes of the world.

He also said in a letter in 1676 that if he was able to see further than his predecessors it was by 'standing on the shoulders of giants.' Those words of Newton's were used in 1998 when a new £2 coin was minted and you can read it round the rim. I think Newton was quoting from Bernard of Chartres who used the phrase earlier in 1130, saying that we are like dwarfs on the shoulders of giants, thus being able to see further than they.

May 6th

The following psalm of David is wonderfully poetic about God's world. Cosmologists can easily point out the errors of early belief in the movement of the sun, but as Lev Landau, a Soviet physicist has cynically said, 'Cosmologists themselves seem to be often in error, but never appear to be in doubt.' Another cynic has said, 'There's speculation; there's pure speculation; and then there's cosmology.'

Let us rejoice at the mysteries and wonders of God's creation as we ponder the following words.

The heavens declare the glory of God,
 the skies proclaim the work of his hands.
Day after day they pour forth speech,
 night after night they display knowledge.
There is no speech or language where their voice is not heard,
Their voice goes out into all the earth,
 their words to the end of the world.

In the heavens he has pitched a tent for the sun
 which is like a bridegroom coming forth from his pavilion,
 like a champion rejoicing to run his course.
It rises at one end of the heavens and makes its circuit to the other,
 nothing is hidden from its heat.

The law of the Lord is perfect, reviving the soul.
The statutes of the Lord are trustworthy, making wise the simple
The precepts of the Lord are right, giving joy to the heart.
The commands of the Lord are radiant, giving light to the eyes.

Psalm 19: 1-8

May 7th

A Celtic Night Prayer

O God of life, this night
 Please darken not to me your light.
O God of life, this night
 Please hide not your gladness from my sight.
O God of light, this night
 Your door to me, please shut not tight
O God of light, this night.

May 8th

Early in January 1998, the first mission for 25 years was going to the moon to explore the poles of the moon to see if there was any water there. I heard then a most touching human story which gave me an added interest in the Lunar Prospector launch. One of the scientists Dr. Eugene Shoemaker had a principal part in training the astronauts in lunar geology. All his life he wanted to go to the moon to 'bang on it with his own hammer', but he never was able to achieve this because of a health problem. He dedicated his knowledge to training those who were fit to go, but before the launch of Lunar Prospector he was killed in a road accident at Alice Springs in Australia.

One of his colleagues, Professor Carolyn Porco of the Lunar Preparatory Laboratory in the University of Arizona had the touching idea of arranging for some of his ashes to be taken on Lunar Prospector. Because of the necessity of keeping the weight low, she could only arrange for one ounce which filled a small cartridge about the size of a lipstick container. She had it wrapped in brass foil which was engraved with the image of the Hale-Bopp comet which was one of the last heavenly bodies he had watched; a photograph of the crater where he had trained the astronauts; and an inscription from Romeo and Juliet. My guess was that this inscription would be:

> O! here
> Will I set up my everlasting rest
> And shake the yoke of inauspicious stars
> From this world-wearied flesh.

Carolyn Porco put me right and told me that because of the love that Dr. Shoemaker had for his wife, also Carolyn, she had chosen the following:

> And, when he shall die,
> Take him and cut him out in little stars,
> And he will make the face of heaven so fine
> That all the world will be in love with night,
> And pay no worship to the garish sun.

The stories of Space exploration are inspiring stories, but nothing can surpass the true stories of human and Divine love. Shoemaker's spirit will be in a better home than the moon, but often the resting place of a loved one's remains has some significance for those still awaiting a reunion. It has ever been so. In this respect it is interesting to read Genesis 50: 5 onwards.

May 9th

I know not what the future hath
  Of marvel or surprise,
Assured alone that life and death
  His mercy underlies.

I know not where his islands lift
  Their fronded palms in air
I only know I cannot drift
  Beyond his love and care.

John Greenleaf Whittier

May 10th

James Weldon Johnson who wrote The Creation which I have used at the beginning of this month, once wrote an article about the ability of the black man to create something original and artistic and because of his gift of adaptibility to give it universal appeal. He said he was able to do this, not only in America, but in the European countries also. The greatest Russian poet was Pushkin, a man of African descent. His great-great grandfather was a full-blooded African of gigantic size who was a special bodyguard to Peter the Great, and who was ennobled and married one of the ladies of the Russian court. Alexandre Dumas, the French romantic writer, had as his father a black native from the French West Indies. The great English musician Coleridge Taylor had a native-born African for his father.

May 11th

Laurens van der Post has a beautiful story about visiting some Africans in the great Okorongo Swamp. They had made dug-outs, or Makorros as they called them. He wondered where they had learnt the skills. The leader looked pityingly at Van der Post and said, 'The First Spirit gave us the vision and we made the Makorro accordingly.' Then he pointed to some weaver birds making their nests from the long, tasselled papyrus of the swamp, and he spoke:

'See how well they build, but even so, you would not think they went to a mission school to learn how. Both they and we have learnt our craft in the same school.'

May 12th

I love the report of the sermon of the African pastor who said to his flock:

You may not be a florist.
  Am I right about that?
But you must tell them that He's the Rose of Sharon.
You may not be a geologist.
But you must tell them that He's the Rock of Ages.
  You know I'm right about that.
You may not be a doctor
But you must tell them that He's the Great Physician.
  Am I right about that?
You may not be a baker
But you must tell them that He's the Bread of Life.
We all know I'm right about that.

May 13th

Is not this the kind of fasting I have chosen:
  to loose the chains of injustice
    and untie the cords of the yoke,
    to set the oppressed free and break every yoke?
Is it not to share your food with the hungry
  and to provide the poor wanderer with shelter -
    when you see the naked to clothe him,
    and not to turn away from your own flesh and blood?
Then your light will break forth like the dawn,
  and your healing will quickly appear;
    then your righteousness will go before you,
    and the glory of the Lord will be your rearguard.
Then you will call and the Lord will answer,
  you will cry for help, and he will say, Here am I.

Isaiah 58: 6-9

May 14th

This is the last prayer which Martin Luther King prayed when he was leaving his congregation in Montgomery, Alabama to become a Civil Rights leader.

'And now unto him who is able to keep us from falling, and who is able to lift us from the dark valley of despair to the bright mountain of hope; who can transport us from the midnight of desperation to the daybreak of joy; to him be power and authority for ever and ever.'

May 15th

Before the late Professor William Barclay of Glasgow University became a well-known figure on television explaining the Scriptures for the ordinary lay person, I heard him preach once in an Edinburgh Church. I can still recall every word of his talk to the children.

'The fingers of the hand were arguing with each other about which was most important.

The first or forefinger said it was so called because it was invariably the finger used to point people in the right direction. The middle finger said of course it was invariably the longest, and having been made so must be the most important. The third finger of the left hand said that of course it was the most important because tradition had it that it led to the heart and was consequently used for the engagement and wedding rings. But the little finger spoke up and said that when someone was writing an important document the little finger was the one that moved along the page guiding and keeping the hand moving in a straight line.

The thumb listened to all the argument and then said to the four fingers. "Here is a book. Which of you can lift it up?" Each of course tried and failed.

The thumb spoke again. "See what you can do if you put all four fingers together for the task."

Together they tried and failed.

"Right," said the thumb, "Put your fingers together with me and see if you can then lift the book."

Together they tried and succeeded.'

I often think of this little parable, and how individually and even corporately as humans, we try and fail. But united and then joined with God we can know success in any important venture.

May 16th

WORK

Because this is my work, O Lord,
  It must be thine.
Because it is a human task
  It is divine.
Take me and brand me with thy cross
  Thy slave's proud sign.

Studdert Kennedy

May 17th

Researcher to Company Director: How many people work in your office?
Director: Approximately fifty per cent of them!

May 18th

I was talking one day to someone who had experienced some difficulty in writing an absolutely truthful testimonial for someone resolutely idle. Finally she cracked it.

'You will be very fortunate if you succeed in getting this person to work for you.'

May 19th

Someone has said, 'If it's big enough to worry about, it's big enough to pray about.'

John Baillie wrote: Near to losing heart? Are you overcome with labour? Or consumed with hopeless longings? Then won't you take the Lord's advice? Don't try to keep the whole thing pent up within your own heart. Share it with God. Tell him all about it, yes down to the last and absurdest detail.

> Oh, what peace we often forfeit
> Oh, what needless pain we bear
> All because we do not carry
> Everything to God in prayer.

May 20th

So do not fear, for I am with you; do not be dismayed, for I am your God. I will strengthen you and help you; I will uphold you with my righteous right hand. For I am the Lord your God who takes hold of your right hand and says to you, Do not fear; I will help you.

Isaiah 41: 10 & 13

May 21st

Aaronic Blessing (from Numbers 6: 24-26)

> The Lord bless you and keep you;
> The Lord make his face shine upon you
> and be gracious to you;
> The Lord turn his face towards you
> and give you peace.

May 22nd

Most writers know all too well the meaning of writer's block, when the words do not flow as you expect them to. It happens with me if anyone attempts to clean up my working area and tidies away those seemingly senseless scribbles which clearly communicate something to me only.

One writer tells how his editor was impatient with him because he had not met his deadline. The writer said wistfully, 'I haven't been idle! I have been looking for the right word for two whole weeks!'

'What about using *fortnight*?' said his editor caustically.

May 23rd

Book launches have become a modern addition to an author's responsibilities. They were never indulged in when I first was published many years back. One of the very important hints I would give to those embarking on this is to have some pads and pencils handy for people to spell out the names of those to whom the books are to be given.

Monica Dickens had a lovely true story of a book launch in Australia where the accent sometimes defeated her. The purchaser said, 'Emma Chisset' when she reached Monica's table. Monica wrote boldly TO EMMA and then said 'Could you spell CHISSET please?'

Her customer looked at her in bewilderment, and then uttered emphatically, 'I only said, "HOW MUCH IS IT?"' We do not always get such amusement out of our errors, but as Fanny Burney has written a couple of centuries back, 'It's a delightful thing to think of perfection; but it's vastly more amusing to talk of errors and absurdities.'

May 24th

I will not wish you riches
  nor the glow of greatness
But that wheresoe'er you go
Some weary soul may gladden
  at your smile
Some weary heart know sunshine
  for a while
And so your path shall be a track of light
Like angel's footsteps passing through the night. *Anon*

May 25th

Earth is crammed with heaven
and every common bush afire with God
but only he who sees
takes off his shoes

Elizabeth Barrett Browning

May 26th

We must not seek to prolong the tranquil peace which can often envelop us when we are enjoying the beauties of God's world, and which can at times entice us away from the difficult and harsh and even bitter and cruel other world needing our attention. But as C.S. Lewis said, 'the power of unsought strange beauty in the casual hour can build a bridge of light.'

REVELATION

I have seen the scarlet flames of sunset glowing
On the everlasting snows:
I have seen a thousand blue-eyed gentians growing
On the rocks and icy floes:
I have seen the moon its silver light bestowing
On still waters desolate:
I have seen the flooding cataracts go flowing
Down the hills in roaring spate:
I have seen the death-pale hand of sunset sowing
A million stars upon the sky:
I have seen the golden starlight, fading, going,
Where no flowers fade or die:
I have seen the storm-winds rise and gather, blowing
Where no foot of man hath trod:
I have seen the white clouds slowly drift, not knowing
whither,
Have I not seen God?

P. Joshua

May 27th

Here is Henry Vaughan's exposition of Micah 6: 8 and also taking in the commandments in Leviticus 19 and Luke 10: 27

To love our God with all our strength and will,
To covet nothing and devise no ill
Against our neighbours, to procure or do
nothing to others which we would not to

Our very selves: not to revenge our wrong;
To be content with little, not to long
For wealth and greatness; to despise or jeer
No man, and if we be despised, to bear:
To feed the hungry, to hold fast our crown:
To take from others nought, to give our own,
These are his precepts, and alas, in these
What is so hard, but faith can do with ease.

May 28th

Lord, we can only enjoy the feeling of hunger,
when we know we are going to be fed.
Help us to enjoy the deeper feeling of the hunger of the soul,
knowing that you have provided spiritual nourishment.

Lord, we can only enjoy the thirst for pure water,
when we know that it is near and our drouth can be quenched.
Help us to enjoy the thirst of the soul and our deep inner longing for righteousness,
Knowing that you are to us the Water of Life if we welcome your presence.

May 29th

I was sitting contemplating one day a cheap print I had bought years ago of Vincent Van Gogh's 'Sunflowers.' The only time I have ever tried to grow sunflowers was when some charity gave us sunflower seeds to grow, sponsoring the charity by giving a sum for their final height in centimetres. Mine were a complete failure and though I paid up a sum, I was really quite glad my garden wasn't burdened with these flamboyant blooms which I have never really liked very much. So I was wondering and indeed admiring Van Gogh's work more than the actual creation which God made. I was impressed by the concentration and artistic skill which had gone into the formation of the petals. Then, with one of those happy coincidences which occur from time to time, the voice of an expert mathematician came on the radio, enthusing about the laws of nature which had gone into the formation of every sunflower head.

If I remember his words correctly he talked about the constraints of nature within which the laws of the universe operate. There were recurring numbers regarding the seeds - numbers which also concern the spiral on a shell or a pineapple or a cone from a conifer. Also the petals of the sunflower lie at an exact angle - if I remember aright it was 137½ desgrees, and this enables every petal to receive the sun to enable it to flourish. The mathematician said that if these constraints on nature's laws were ignored there would be chaos.

I thought deeply about these two ways of looking with awe at God's creation - the artistic eye of Van Gogh and the scientific one, and neither can exclude the other. I who am neither a scientist nor an artist just look with increasing humility at the many wonders which make up God's world, and I often whisper a thank you.

May 30th

The Everlasting Mercy

Saul Kane's Conversion

O Christ, who holds the open gate
O Christ who drives the furrow straight
O Christ, the plough, O Christ, the laughter
Of holy white birds flying after,
Lo, all my heart's field red and torn,
And thou wilt bring the young green corn,
The young green corn divinely springing,
The young green corn for ever singing;
And when the field is fresh and fair
Thy blessed feet shall glitter there.
And we will walk the weeded field,
And tell the golden harvest's yield,
The corn that makes the holy bread
By which the soul of man is fed,
The holy bread, the food unpriced,
Thy everlasting mercy, Christ.

John Masefield

May 31st

It was a man from the Isle of Lewis who after having the Spanish word *mañana* explained to him looked at his informant wonderingly and then said, 'Here in the islands we have no such word of comparable urgency.'

JUNE

The world is charged with the grandeur of God.
It will flame out......

Gerard Manley Hopkins

June 1st

Lord, for tomorrow and its needs
I do not pray.
Keep me my God from stain of sin
Just for today.
Let me both diligently work
And duly pray.
Let me be kind in word and deed
Just for today.
Let me be slow to do *my* will,
Prompt to obey.
O, keep me in your loving care
Just for today.

Let me no wrong or idle word
Unthinking say.
Set now a seal upon my lips
Just for today.
Let me in season, Lord, be grave
In season gay.
Let me be faithful to your grace
Just for today.

And if today my tide of life should ebb away
Give me, sweet Lord, your sacraments divine.
So, for tomorrow and its needs
I do not pray.
But keep, and guide and love me Lord,
Just for today.

Sybil F. Partridge

June 2nd

D. H. Lawrence said that it was a fearful thing to fall into the hands of the Lord, but it was an even more fearful thing to fall out of them.

June 3rd

My Granny had on her wall the words of Proverbs 15: 1: 'A soft answer turns away wrath.'
When I'm hasty and impetuous they return with force as I pray this little prayer:
'Lord, make my words warm and tender, for I may well have to eat them tomorrow.'

June 4th

Michele Guinness tells a lovely story of a parishioner who said she felt very full of gratitude to her vicar's wife for she had set them such a good example. When the wife inquired what it was that she had particularly done, the parishioner floored her by saying that she had been the first one to have the courage to attend church wearing coloured tights!

When I was the very new bride of a minister in the North of Scotland, one old lady looked me up and down and almost through and through. Then she turned to my husband and said to him, 'It wasnae guid looks ye married, onyway!' She wasn't much of an oil painting herself, and I waited for my Sir Galahad to come to my rescue. All that he said was, 'Never mind, Elizabeth. You'll wear well!'

June 5th

FABLE

by Ralph Waldo Emerson

The mountain and the squirrel
  Had a quarrel.
And the former called the latter, 'Little prig!'
Bun replied,
  'You are doubtless very big;
But all sorts of things and weather
Must be taken in together,
  To make up a year
  And a sphere.
And I think it no disgrace
To occupy my place.
If I'm not so large as you
You are not so small as I
  And not half as spry.

I'll not deny you make
A very pretty squirrel track;
Talents differ; all is well and wisely put;
If I cannot carry forests on my back,
Neither can you crack a nut."

June 6th

Moses said to God, 'Who am I, that I should go to Pharaoh and bring the Israelites out of Egypt?'

And God said, 'I will be with you.'

Moses said to the Lord, 'O Lord, I have never been eloquent, neither in the past nor since you have spoken to your servant. I am slow of speech and tongue.'

The Lord said to him, 'Who gave man his mouth? Who makes him deaf or mute? Who gives him sight or makes him blind? Is it not I, the Lord? Now go. I will help you speak and will teach you what to say.'

Exodus 3: 11 & 12a and Exodus 4: 10-12

June 7th

When we are suffering the heat of someone's anger, be it just or unjust,
shade us from the scorching.
When we are suffering the iciness of someone's rejection,
shelter us from the cold blast.
When we are suffering from the darkness of misunderstanding,
shine on us with your light.
When we are suffering from the weakness and fatigue of the journey,
be to us a strong staff and support.
When we are suffering from the becalmment of lethargy and indifference,
send us the strong wind of your Spirit.

You are the answer to all our needs.
Stay with us always
So that we see your face
And know your power.

Whatever the circumstances, we welcome your presence.

June 8th

I read an extraordinary story some time ago about a bookseller who specialised in selling theological works and who had great difficulty in preventing clergy stealing his stock. The shop was like a warren of book-lined rooms. Some of the thieves he caught red-handed and they pleaded absent mindedness or guilt but asked not to be reported to the police. He said that he had put up a large sign with the commandment 'Thou shalt not steal' in large letters, but it was just ignored. Then, just for fun, he put up a curse that he had found, which originates in the San Pedro Monastery in Barcelona.

'For him that stealeth a Book from this Library, let it change into a serpent in his hand and rend him. Let him be struck with Palsy and all his Members blasted. Let him languish in Pain crying aloud for Mercy and let there be no sur-cease to his agony till he sink in Dissolution. Let Bookwormes gnaw his Entrails in token of the Worm that dieth not, and when at last he goeth to his final Punishment, let the flames of Hell consume him for ever and aye.'

The curse had a dramatic effect, one vicar returning anonymously a parcel of 40 books which he had stolen over a period of six months. The bookseller was astonished that what he had regarded as as a humorous ploy on his part had achieved such success in restraining the shop-lifters. The bookseller in question is now searching for a similar spell which would make people *buy* his books!

A curious bit of information came to light after this report of the effect of the San Pedro Curse. One employee of the Crown Courts Circuit Library said that the same Curse is displayed there too, but the effect on lawyers does not appear to be the same as on the clergy.

June 9th

G.K. Chesterton said that he acknowledged that he could not always practise what he preached, but God forbid that he should be required to preach what he practised!

Dylan Thomas has given us some lovely words in the Sunset Prayer of Rev. Eli Jenkins in Under Milkwood.

> We are not wholly bad or good
> Who live our lives under Milkwood
> And Thou I know wilt be the first
> To see our best side not our worst.

This reliance on the grace of God does not absolve us from our misdeeds, but encourages us to acknowledge them and to seek true repentance, which means a turning away from them in order to accept forgiveness.

June 10th

I am always interested in the origins of sayings which have become commonplace in our language. When I was writing the story of the thieving clergy I nearly used the expression, 'They were chancing their arm.' It is not really an appropriate expression to cover what is really trying to get away with downright theft for it has come to mean taking a risk of some kind which will bring profit in the end. I believe its origins are in St. Patrick's Cathedral in Dublin where during a dispute long ago, those fleeing from trouble took refuge in part of the building. A hole was bored through a door so that an arm could be reached towards the enemy as an offer of reconciliation. When the hand was clasped and shaken, a truce was called. But of course, the chancing of the arm meant that it could be hacked off instead by the enemy.

June 11th

I wonder how the clergy in the bookstore satisfied their conscience. Louis MacNeice has a poem about The British Museum Reading Room where he refers to the walls of books and the readers who are there for varying reasons. Maybe the guilty clergy were like those who hoped that the walls of books would 'deaden the drumming of the demon in their ears.' Or were they like those 'asleep, hanging like bats in a world of inverted values?'

We used to refer to ourselves as 'miserable sinners' and having 'contrite hearts' and we acknowledged the fatal flaws in our characters which needed God's attention and help. Not so much today, when it is the broad trend to denigrate achievement and sling mud at one-time icons, for we almost enjoy hearing that our idols have feet of clay. There are constantly snide remarks about the 'squeaky clean.' Yet there is still the custom in Britain that you cannot put up a statue to anyone until ten years after his death. By then the truth should be clearer, when what has come to be known as 'spin-doctoring,' or distorting the real picture will be less.

June 12th

I wish I loved the human race;
I wish I loved its silly face;
I wish I liked the way it walks;
I wish I liked the way it talks;
And when I'm introduced to one
I wish I thought *What Jolly Fun*!

Walter Raleigh (1923)

June 13th

Who is wise and understanding among you? Let him show it by his good life, by deeds done in the humility that comes from wisdom. But if you harbour bitter envy and selfish ambitions in your hearts, do not boast about it or deny the truth. Such wisdom does not come down from heaven but is earthly, unspiritual, of the devil. For where you have envy and selfish ambition, there you will find disorder and every evil practice. But the wisdom that comes from heaven is first of all pure; then peace-loving, considerate, submissive, full of mercy and good fruit, impartial and sincere. Peacemakers who sow in peace raise a harvest of righteousness.

James 3: 13 -18

June 14th

Lord, Grant us never to parley with temptation, never to tamper with conscience; never to spare the right eye, or hand or foot that is a snare to us; never to lose our souls, though in exchange we should gain the whole world.

Christina Rossetti

June 15th

There are books which stay in the mind and heart long after you first read them. I first read 'My Lady Of The Chimney Corner' when I was still a pupil at my Ulster school and living not far from Antrim where Alexander Irvine and his mother Anna and father Jamie had earlier had their humble home in Pogue's Entry. One day Anna was talking to Willie Witheroe who was the stone-breaker in the district and she startled him by telling him that she had seen and entertained the Son of Man every day of her life. She said she'd made tea for him and broth on Sunday and she'd mended his old clothes and said kind words to him. Willie thought Anna was going mad but Anna showed him her

Bible and read to him, translating into his language, 'When ye do it t'wan o' these craithers ye do it t' Me.'

Willie Witheroe had reason to remember these words when he was confronted one day by a local woman of ill repute. He told her there was nothing she could do for him, but if he could give her something he would. He was going to roast a dozen potatoes on his fire and have them with a drink of buttermilk. He told the woman she could have six of the potatoes when he had finished and was leaving the place.

He was feeling pleased with his new-found generosity until he thought he could hear the voice of Anna.

'So, you have the Son of Man to dinner today?'

Willie was gratified at this recognition until he seemed to hear Anna again.

'And you're giving him your leavings?'

He was cut to the quick and ran after the woman of ill repute and told her to come and eat as much as she wanted first and he would take what was left. And he told her the story that Anna had told him about the Son of Man. Willie never saw the woman again, but before she died later in the poor-house she sent word to Willie that the Son of Man had visited her in the ward and that she was content to die.

June 16th

Anna Irvine was a wonderful expositor of the Scriptures, but she said wisely one day that if there was one thing that this world needed more than any other, it was an undisputed text. She said that the mortal pity of it is that Christians often use texts only as pins to stick in each other's flesh.

June 17th

I sought my soul
  But my soul I could not see
I sought my God
  But my God eluded me
I sought my brother
  And I found all three

Anon

June 18th

Anna Irvine had a wonderful sense of humour and her son Alexander tells how she dealt with Willie Witheroe one never- to-be-forgotten night when he had dropped in for shelter from the snow and the howling wind. Poverty meant that there was not always peat on the fire or a boiling kettle waiting for the ration of tea, in Jamie and Anna's house. Their second child had indeed died of starvation. But this night the kettle hung on the chain, singing. Willie who was a philosopher, cynic and humorist used one of his hints that generally brought results.

'I suppose you boil the water for tomorrow's tea, Anna, the night before?'

Anna answered adroitly, 'Oh no, Willie, Sufficient unto the day is the evil thereof. We have the tea the night before, and just use our imaginations the following morning!'

But Willie got his cup of tea, for Jamie declared if he didn't, he'd wind up by scalding his throat with boiling water.

June 19th

Anna Irvine's motto was 'Love is enough' and those who were the richer for living in her presence knew how often this proved true. They also alas, at times knew and suffered from a different kind of charity described by John Boyle O'Reilly all too aptly.

> Organised charity, scrimped and iced
> In the name of a cautious, statistical Christ.

It behoves us to search our own hearts when we attempt to help those who need a crust or a kind word.

June 20th

Each helps the other and says to his brother, 'Be strong!'
The craftsman encourages the goldsmith, and he who smooths with the hammer, spurs on him who strikes the anvil.
He says of the welding, 'It is good.'.......
I have chosen you and have not rejected you.
So, do not fear, for I am with you, do not be dismayed, for I am your God.
I will strengthen you and help you;
I will uphold you with my righteous right hand.

Isaiah 41: 6-7 & 9-10

June 21st

Lord make us true servants to all those in need
Filled with compassion in thought, word and deed
Loving our neighbour, whatever the cost
Feeding the hungry and finding the lost.

Lord, make us healers of body and mind
Give us the power to give sight to the blind
Love to the loveless and gladness for pain
Filling all hearts with the joy of your name.

One Worship

June 22nd

Some time ago a party of enthusiasts were heading off to the Caribbean to see a total solar eclipse which would last only four minutes. I listened to an astronomer talking about their journey and he said he deplored the fact that they were all laden with cameras. He wished they would just savour the few moments of the eclipse without blocking it out by trying to capture a photograph. For himself, he said the emotional memory of such a beautiful moment would last longer than any photo.

Practically the only people in that Western world not watching the eclipse were the Wayuu Indians in Venezuela and Colombia. They averted their eyes in the belief that the sun and moon were making love in order to create new stars.

June 23rd

'There are tourists incapable of looking at a masterpiece for its own sake. They bow into a camera, snap experiences they've never had, then rush home and develop the celluloid events, so as to see where they've been.'

Ned Boram

June 24th

'When I was a boy of fourteen, my father was so ignorant that I could not bear to have the old man around. When I got to be twenty-one, I was surprised at how much the old man had learnt in the intervening years.'

Mark Twain

June 25th

A bishop went to speak to students at Yale University. He used an acrostic on YALE:

Y for Youth; A for Ambition: L for Loyalty: E for Energy.

The sermon took half an hour and one student was heard to comment, 'Thank God our university isn't in Massachusetts.'

As Churchill once said, 'The head cannot take in more than the seat can endure.'

June 26th

If you have a pain in the neck, thank God you are not a giraffe.

June 27th

Do we need, like some people, letters of recommendation to you or from you? You yourselves are our letter, written on our hearts, known and read by everybody. You show that you are a letter from Christ, the result of our ministry, written not with ink but with the Spirit of God, not on tablets of stone but on tablets of the human heart.

2 Corinthians 3: 1-3

June 28th

From the cowardice
  that dare not face new truth:
From the laziness
  that is contented with half-truth:
From the arrogance
  that thinks it knows all truth
Good Lord, deliver us.

African Prayer

June 29th

An author called Susan Ertz had in one of her novels a letter to one of the characters who was indisposed.

Dear Stephen,

I am so sorry you are feeling less well. How is the phlebitis? No one should suffer from anything with such a pretty name. Did you ever stop to think that the names of diseases and the names of flowers are very similar? For instance, I might say, 'Do come and see my garden. It's at its best now and the double pneumonias are really wonderful. I suppose the mild winters had something to do with that. I am very proud of my trailing phlebitis too and the laryngitises and deep-purple quinsies that I put in last year are a joy to behold. The bed of asthmas and malarias that you used to admire is finer than ever this summer, and the dear little dropsies are all in bloom down by the lake and make such a pretty showing with the blue of the anthrax border behind them.'

June 30th

The Vagaries of the English Language

Have you ever endeavoured
To pronounce revered and severed
Demon, lemon, ghoul, foul, soul,
Peter, petrol and patrol?
Billet does not end like ballet:
Bouquet, wallet, mallet, chalet.
Blood and flood are not like food.
Nor is mould like would and should......
Hiccough has the sound of SUP.......
My advice is: GIVE IT UP!

Gerard N. Trenite

JULY

To me the meanest flower that blows can give
Thoughts that do often lie too deep for tears

William Wordsworth

July 1st

TODAY

So here hath been dawning
Another blue day
Think, will you let it
Slip useless away?

Out of eternity
This new day is born;
Into eternity
All night will return

Behold it aforetime
No eye ever did;
So soon it forever
From all eyes is hid

Here hath been dawning
Another blue day
Think, will you let it
Slip useless away?

Thomas Carlyle

July 2nd

A great many people think they are thinking, when they are really just re-arranging their prejudices.

William James

July 3rd

The husband was continually immersed in his newspaper, and the wife becoming increasingly exasperated. Finally, she shouted, 'When *are* you going to learn that there's far more to life than what's going on in the world?'

July 4th

I kept six honest serving men
They served me all I knew
Their names were WHAT and WHY and WHEN
And HOW and WHERE and WHO.

July 5th

Mark Twain once said, 'It ain't those parts of the Bible that I can't understand that bother me, it is the parts that I do understand.' I wonder if he was paraphrasing what Goethe said in an earlier generation, albeit in a more erudite way.

Dean Swift had a rhyme asserting our indebtedness to others for the thoughts we often believe are our own originals.

> So, naturalists observe, a flea
> Hath smaller fleas that on him prey;
> And these have smaller fleas to bite 'em,
> And so proceed *ad infinitum.*
> Thus every poet, in his kind,
> Is bit by him that comes behind.

July 6th

Not many of you were wise by human standards; not many were influential; not many were of noble birth. But God chose the foolish things of the world to shame the wise; God chose the weak things of the world to shame the strong. He chose the lowly things of the world and the despised things - and the things that are not - to nullify the things that are, so that no-one may boast before him. It is because of him that you are in Christ Jesus, who has become for us wisdom from God - that is our righteousness, holiness and redemption.

1 Corinthians 1: 26-30

July 7th

> O Lord Jesus Christ,
> who are as a great rock in a weary land
> who beholds your weak creatures
> weary of labour, weary of pleasure,
> weary of hope deferred; weary of self;
> in your abundant compassion,
> and fellow-feeling with us,
> and unutterable tenderness,
> bring us we pray you,
> unto our rest.

Christina Rossetti

July 8th

There was a skit done some years back on TV by the Two Ronnies, when they had their own Mastermind General Knowledge Programme, Ronnie Barker being a stand-in for Magnus Magnusson, the questioner, and Ronnie Corbett being the contestant. The humour involved Ronnie Corbett giving all the right answers, but in the wrong order.

The sketch reminded me of my Ulster childhood, when we all sat in serried ranks in our classrooms awaiting the annual descent of the church ministers in the area to examine us in Religious Instruction as it was then called. Was it instruction, education or indoctrination? Things were learnt very often by rote, and it was only much later I knew what it was to learn by heart, a vastly more worthy exercise.

Later, at the time of my entry to the classroom as a teacher, this annual visit of the clergy was still taking place, and the only good thing about it was that after they departed, we all got the rest of the day off. An experienced teacher told me not to be too hasty about coaching my young pupils in the answers, for disasters had been known to occur. One teacher coached each pupil in what should be his answer knowing she was to have an elderly minister, who always started at the front right hand side, working along the row with the questions of the catechism, Just as the examination was about to start, the first pupil asked to be excused.

The minister commenced and asked pupil number two the first question, 'Who made you?'

Undaunted, the boy gave him the answer, 'Man's chief end is to glorify God and enjoy him forever.'

'No! no!' said the minister testily, 'When I ask you, "Who made you?" you should answer, "God made me."'

'But,' replied the offended pupil, since he'd learnt his line too well, 'The boy that God made has gone to the toilet.'

July 9th

Better to keep your mouth shut and appear stupid, than open it and remove all doubt.

Mark Twain

From all my lame defeats and oh! much more
From all the victories that I seemed to score;
From cleverness shot forth on Thy behalf
At which while angels weep, the audience laugh;
From all my proofs of Thy divinity
Thou, who wouldst give no sign, deliver me.....
Lord of the narrow gate and the needle's eye,
Take from me all my trumpery lest I die.

'The Apologist's Evening Prayer' by C.S. Lewis

July 10th

Do the work that's nearest, though it's dull at whiles
Helping, when you meet them, lame dogs over stiles.

July 11th

Having written what has gone before and my experience of primary school religious affairs, I am immediately reminded of a different experience which Seamus Deane had. He relates it in his autobiographical novel 'Reading In The Dark.' It was a troubled time of distrust and revenge in Deane's native town of Derry and the priest was in the school trying to prevent the pupils following the years-old traditions of hatred and violence.

'It is not for us to judge. It is for us to see the difference between the wrong done *to* us, and equal wrong done *by* us; to know our transient life, no matter how scarred, how miserable it might be, is also God's miracle and gift: that we may try to improve it, but we may not destroy it. If we destroy it in another, we destroy it in ourselves......'

July 12th

The man who wants to get his revenge should be told he must make sure to dig two graves.

Old Chinese Proverb

July 13th

There is to my mind, no more beautiful passage in the Authorised Version of the Bible than 1 Corinthians: 13. It cannot be bettered, but sometimes I like to read the paraphrasing of it in Christopher Wordsworth's hymn.

Gracious Spirit, Holy Ghost,
Taught by you, we covet most,
Of your gifts at Pentecost,
  Holy, heavenly love.

Faith that mountains could remove,
Tongues of earth or heaven above,
Knowledge, all things, empty prove
  Without heavenly love.

Though I as a martyr bleed,
Give my goods the poor to feed,
All is vain if love I need;
  Therefore give me love.

Love is kind, and suffers long;
Love is meek and thinks no wrong
Love in death itself more strong;
  Therefore give us love.

Prophecy will fade away
Melting in the light of day
Love will ever with us stay;
  Therefore give us love.

Faith and hope and love we see,
Joining hand in hand, agree;
But the greatest of the three,
  And the best is love.

July 14th

Old Celtic Prayer (adapted)

May the God who guided Noah over the flood waves
  guide me through the troubled waters.
May the God who recalled Jonah from the deep
  deliver me from my darkness.
May the Christ who stretched forth his hand to Peter as
    he was sinking
  rescue me from my failure.
O God, you did marvellous things in days of old.
Do some marvellous things in our time also.

July 15th

Gilbert White was an English clergyman living from 1720 until 1793, what appeared to be a largely uneventful life in Selborne, Hampshire. He is buried in an obscure part of the cemetery there and all that is on his tombstone are the initials G.W. Yet his fame has far outlasted his years of obscurity, for he wrote a book called 'Natural History and Antiquities of Selborne' which has become a classic. It took him a twenty year period to write the letters on which it was based and White's Thrush is named after him. White said that his pet tortoise, called Timothy, could read the weather better than any human. Like many a tortoise Timothy lived longer than his master, or to be correct, her master. Despite all his knowledge, Gilbert White did not know that he had misnamed Timothy, for after his death, the tortoise was discovered to be female. I find this lack of knowledge somehow part of Gilbert White's attraction.

As Mignon McLaughlin has said, 'It's innocence when it charms us and ignorance when it doesn't'.

July 16th

Democracy is the recurrent suspicion that more than half of the people are right more than half of the time.

E.B. White

July 17th

Lord Tonypandy - George Thomas - was Speaker of the House of Commons from 1976 until 1982. He was known as a man of firm faith, sure hope, deep humanity and unfailing good humour. One day an MP was demanding an emergency debate on some subject or other, and he maintained that the subject in question was in every paper that day.

'So is my horoscope!' said Mr. Speaker Thomas as he dismissed the request.

July 18th

I suppose we all have our travel tales of the vagaries of our rail system. The passengers on a train soon after privatisation were astonished to hear the guard's announcement, 'I would like to point out to passengers that this train is on time.'

There is a record held of a London bus timetable of more than half a century ago which had the following disclaimer:

'The Board does not undertake nor shall be deemed to undertake, that vehicles will run at the time specified - or at all.'

July 19th

He is a path, if any be misled;
He is a robe, if any naked be;
If any chance to hunger, he is bread;
If any be a bondman, he is free;
If any be but weak, how strong is he!
  To any dead men life he is, to sick men health;
  To any blind men sight, and to the needy wealth,
A pleasure without loss, a treasure without stealth.

Giles Fletcher

July 20th

Do not throw away your confidence, it will be richly rewarded. You need to persevere so that when you have done the will of God, you will receive what he has promised. He who is coming will come and will not delay....
Now faith is being sure of what we hope for and certain of what we do not see. This is what the ancients were commended for.

Hebrews 10: 35-37 & 11: 1-2

July 21st

O God, too near to be found: too simple to be conceived: too good to be believed: help us to trust not in our knowledge of you, but in your knowledge of us: to be certain of you, not because we feel our thoughts of you are true, but because we know you far transcend them.

May we not be anxious just to discern your will, but content rather with desire to do it. May we not strain our minds to understand your nature so much as to yield ourselves and live our lives only to express you.

Show us how foolish it is to doubt you, since you yourself set the very questions that disturb us. Reveal our unbelief to be faith fretting at its outward form. Be gracious when we want to cease from moral strife. Reveal what it is that struggles in us. Before we tire of mental search, enable us to see that it was not ourselves but your call which stirred our souls.

Turn us back from our voyages of thought to that which sent us forth. Teach us to trust not in cleverness or learning, but to that inward faith which can never be denied. Lead us out of all confusion to simplicity. Call us back from wandering without to find you at home within.

W.E. Orchard

July 22nd

When we were still a complete family with just the usual childish ailments and normal winter illnesses, and both my husband and myself, though not well-off, were a secure and happy pair, my husband preached on the subject 'What will you do when the props give way?' He had often said to me that he hoped the congregation would not consider him presumptuous when he tried to speak about coping with adversity - grief, sorrow, crippling illness, terrible anxiety. He would always follow his preparation for such a sermon by saying to me that he trusted if we were ever called upon to suffer any great trouble we would be able to hold on to the beliefs which he was trying to convey to his flock. He was sure it was a tremendous help to know and believe the promises of God before the time came to have to rely on them wholeheartedly.

When he preached on 'What will you do when the props give way?' he said, 'Health can deteriorate with alarming suddenness. Riches can take wings and fly away. Friends and loved ones are removed far from us ..... If we are to survive the destruction of these props, if we are to endure to the end, then God must do something for us ......'

I came to think of that as a prophetic sermon for it was shortly afterwards he suddenly became mortally ill and every earthly prop was removed. Did then God do something for us? It's only in retrospect that we can see the picture being completed and realise how many times a door was closed, but after some darkness and bewilderment a window was opened; how one has had to learn the language of suffering - that though time is a healer, one has to learn to live with the scars; that to accept time's healing capacity is no betrayal, but rather a moving on in letting the earthly props go. This becomes easier with age as we realise we are walking the Western road where we know we are nearing the place where our heart will in God's good time eventually lay down its load.

To have, to love, to lose - and then again to find.

July 23rd

The props assist the house
Until the house is built
And then the props withdraw -
And adequate, erect,
The house supports itself;
Ceasing to recollect
The auger and the carpenter.
Just such a retrospect
Hath the perfected life,
A past of plank and nail,
And slowness - then the scaffolds drop -
Affirming it a soul.

Emily Dickinson

July 24th

Anna Irvine of 'My Lady of the Chimney Corner' fame was comforting a neighbour, Eliza Lecky, on the death of her husband. She said that when the spirit leaves the body, we say the body's dead, but it's just like a partnership gone broke. One goes up and one goes down. And Anna followed this by saying she didn't believe in kissing a corpse, for to her it was like kissing a bird's cage when the bird had escaped - *there's nothing in it!*

July 25th

Some of you say, 'Joy is greater than sorrow,' and others say, 'Nay, sorrow is the greater.'

But I say unto you, they are inseparable.

Together they come, and when one sits alone with you at your board, remember then that the other is asleep on your bed.

Verily you are suspended like scales between your sorrow and your joy.

Only when you are empty are you at a standstill and balanced.

When the treasurekeeper lifts you to weigh his gold and his silver, needs must your joy or your sorrow rise or fall.

Kahlil Gibran

July 26th

If I should go before the rest of you
Break not a flower nor inscribe a stone,
Nor when I'm gone speak in a Sunday voice
But be the usual selves that I have known.
Weep if you must
Parting is hell,
But life goes on,
So sing as well.

Joyce Grenfell

July 27th

They shall hunger no more,
Neither thirst any more;
Neither shall the sun light on them,
Nor any heat.

For the Lamb which is in the midst of the throne
shall feed them,
And shall lead them into living fountains of waters;
And God shall wipe away all tears from their eyes.

Revelation 7: 16-17 (AV)

July 28th

The following prayer was written by someone close to me, a few years after her husband had been killed by the IRA. She had witnessed the killing and had gone through a period of questioning the omnipotence and the benevolence of a loving God. Then she found that suffering could be redemptive.

O God, take all my sins and forgive them.
Take all my sorrows and use them.
Take all my disappointments and frustrated hopes
and make of them a stairway to yourself.
Take all of me which is imperfect and broken
but which in your love becomes whole.
I ask this through Jesus Christ our Lord
whose life was made a sacrament
and whose Cross became a throne.

Amen

July 29th

When questioned once, D.L. Moody replied, 'Well, yes, I have been filled with the Holy Spirit. But sadly, sometimes I leak!'

Don't we all?

July 30th

There are some strange sayings in the Bible which one can only understand, if someone explains what life was like in Biblical times and in Biblical lands. I had absolutely no idea of the meaning of 'I am become like a bottle in the smoke', which is from Psalm 119: 83, until a biblical scholar explained that when a leather wineskin was filled with wine it was hung by a fire until the skin became tough and hard and gnarled, whilst all the time the wine within was maturing. The very appearance of the outside would indicate the wine within was rich and ready. This also throws light on the teaching in Matthew 9: 17 when Jesus said that new wine had to be put into new wineskins if it was to be preserved.

There is something which seems very curious to me about the influence of the Bible on the ascending sizes of bottles of wine. The equivalent of 4 bottles of wine (3 litres) was named after Jeroboam, the first king of the northern Kingdom of Israel. 6 bottles are called after Rehoboam, Solomon's son and successor as King of Judah. Methuselah, the longest lived man, and grandfather of Noah is for 8 bottles. Then back to kings, and this time kings of Assyria and Babylon. Salmanazar is for 12 bottles; Balthazar for 16 bottles and Nebuchadnezzar for 20 bottles.

July 31st

Here is a radio conversation released by the Chief of Naval Operations on October 15th, 1995. It was between an American naval ship and Canadian authorities off the coast of Newfoundland.

Americans: Please divert your course 15 degrees to the North to avoid a collision.

Canadians: Recommend you divert course 15 degrees to the South to avoid a collision.

Americans: This is the captain of a US Navy ship. I say again, divert course.

Canadians: NO! I say again, divert course.

Americans: THIS IS THE AIRCRAFT CARRIER USS ABRAHAM LINCOLN, THE SECOND LARGEST SHIP IN THE UNITED NATIONS ATLANTIC FLEET. WE ARE ACCOMPANIED BY THREE DESTROYERS, THREE CRUISERS AND NUMEROUS SUPPORT VESSELS. I DEMAND THAT YOU CHANGE YOUR COURSE 15 DEGREES NORTH, THAT IS ONE FIVE DEGREES NORTH, OR COUNTER MEASURES WILL BE UNDERTAKEN TO ENSURE THE SAFETY OF THIS SHIP.

Canadians: This is a lighthouse. Your call.

With patience first, and patience last
and doggedness all through,
A man can think the wildest thoughts
and make them all come true.

Unattributed

AUGUST

The whole world was full of wonders
Too many to put down now....
William Langland (Piers Plowman)

August 1st

I worship you, sweet will of God
And all your ways adore
And every day I live, I long
To love you more and more.

I have no cares, O blessed Will!
For all my cares are shared
I live in triumph, Lord, for you
My anxious prayers have heard.

Ride on, ride on, triumphantly
O, glorious will, ride on:
Faith's pilgrim folk behind you take
The road that you have gone.

He always wins who sides with God
To him no chance is lost:
God's will is sweetest to him when
It triumphs at his cost.

Ill that he blesses is our good
And unblest good is ill:
And all is right that seems most wrong
If it be his sweet will.

F.W. Faber (adapted)

August 2nd

Q. What is the difference between ignorance and apathy?
A. I don't know and I don't care.

August 3rd

Famous Seamus - Seamus Heaney the Irish poet - won prizes including the Whitbread Book of the Year Prize and in 1995 the Nobel Prize for Literature. Once he said that all the rewards he had received were as nothing compared to 'the self-delighting satisfaction of just writing something that is worthwhile.'

Another prizewinner, Noureddine Morceli, at the 1996 Olympic Games won a medal for the 1500 metres race. Afterwards he said, 'The records and medals are wonderful, but they're more trinkets in reality. They cannot feed all the people in the world who are hungry, clothe all those who are cold, comfort all those who are troubled, or bring peace to all those who are at war.'

August 4th

Bernard Shaw was famous for many things, and not least for declining the offer of putting his name on the Honours list. When he refused, he said, 'Just being Bernard Shaw is honour enough!' It was also Bernard Shaw who said, 'Those who can, do. Those who can't, teach.'

We who were in the profession extended that by saying, 'And those who can't teach, teach the teachers. And those who can't teach the teachers become Directors of Education - or even Inspectors of Schools. They might even become ministers of Education.'

August 5th

The mediocre teacher tells. The good teacher explains. The superior teacher demonstrates. The great teacher inspires.

William Arthur Ward

August 6th

When he had finished washing their feet, he put on his clothes and returned to his place.

'Do you understand what I have done for you?' he asked them. 'You called me "Teacher" and "Lord" and rightly so, for that is what I am. Now that I, your Lord and Teacher, have washed your feet, you should also wash one another's feet. I have set you an example that you should do as I have done for you. I tell you the truth, no servant is greater than his master, nor is a messenger greater than him that sent him. Now that you know these things, you will be blest if you do them.'

John 13: 12-17

August 7th

Prayer For Discernment

Grant me, O Lord, to know what is worth knowing
To love what is worth loving,
To praise what delights you most,
To value what is precious in your sight,
To hate what is offensive to you.
Do not let me judge by what I see,
nor pass sentence according to what I hear,
but to judge rightly between things that differ,
and above all to search out and to do what pleases you,
through Jesus Christ our Lord.

Thomas à Kempis

August 8th

A great many books written by Irish writers about their childhood experiences have hit the headlines in recent years - Home Before Night by Hugh Leonard; Reading In The Dark by Seamus Deane; Angela's Ashes by Frank McCourt; and others. They have all helped to evoke my own childhood experiences, resurrecting old memories and the impressions they left on me. I have very fond memories of my primary school teachers and the love they gave me at a very early age for poetry and music. I left Primary when I was eleven to go on a scholarship to the local Grammar School but already I had been introduced to Pythagoras, to Gray's Elegy In A Country Churchyard and the like, and not least I was taught how to sight read vocal music from both staff notation and tonic solfa. That was our head-master's forte, and I remember him as a gifted teacher, with all too obvious frailties outside school - the kind of indulgences which are known to do harm to the liver. But we loved him.

When some of us were leaving his care to go to higher education, as I felt it was sometimes mistakenly described, we wanted to buy him a little gift from our pocket money. So at lunch time one day we set off to a small specialist shop where the window displayed many little trinkets we thought suitable for him. A democratic decision had to be made on which item to buy, and this took more time than we had bargained for. When we heard the school bell in the distance we ran back as fast as we could, but realised by now we had committed a dire sin in trying to do our shopping at that time. So as we entered the head's classroom where the rest had already embarked on the afternoon lesson, he lined us up. We were going to be made an example to the other non-school-leavers. I have no doubt he thought we were becoming arrogant in our approach to primary school discipline.

He lifted the cane, and starting at one end of the line he said, 'Why were you not in school on time?'

Each one gave the same answer, 'We had to go to the shops, Sir.' And each got a whack on the left hand. That is until he came to the last pupil who had been chosen to hand over the gift.

'Why were you not in school on time?'

'Because we were buying this for you, Sir!'

We were as demolished as he was when we saw his face crumple, and his eyes become misty, and his voice hoarse, as he whispered, 'Why didn't you say so at the beginning?'

It was chastening for us to realise that we had caused a strong man to cry, and as we went to our seats, we nursed a smarting left hand but no grudges. We were a silent and obedient class as we got out our books and worked quietly away at an exercise he had scribbled on the board for us. He sat quietly at his desk, head in hands, and I wouldn't be surprised if all he desperately wanted at that moment was a glass of his favourite tipple.

I learnt more than one lesson that day and not least what it is to be wounded by your own understanding of love. I also knew in my own childish way that you cannot 'lay remorse on the innocent nor lift it from the heart of the guilty.'

August 9th

The Village Schoolmaster

Beside yon straggling fence that skirts the way,
With blossomed furze unprofitably gay,
There, in his noisy mansion, skilled to rule,
The village master taught his little school;
A man severe he was and stern to view,
I knew him well, and every truant knew;
Well had the boding tremblers learned to trace
The day's disasters in his morning face.
Full well they laughed with counterfeited glee
At all his jokes, for many a joke had he;
Full well the busy whispering, circling round
Conveyed the dismal tidings when he frowned;

Yet he was kind, or if severe in aught,
The love he bore to learning was in fault.

....

And still they gazed, and still the wonder grew
That one small head could carry all he knew.

Oliver Goldsmith

August 10th

I was angry with my friend
I told my wrath, my wrath did end.
I was angry with my foe
I told it not, my wrath did grow.

William Blake

August 11th

Harold Pinter told a lovely story when he accepted the David Cohen British Literary Award in 1993. He recalled what he described as one of the most interesting and indeed acute questions in a career attended by a great deal of dramatic criticism. He had been at a book-signing session when a mother with her 6 year old son came along. She said to her son, introducing Pinter, 'This man is a very good writer.' The boy looked at him in admiration for a moment and then asked his mother, 'Can he do a W?'

When I think of the joy of pupils when they have done something difficult for the first time, I remember hearing someone say that the best leaders are those who when they have finished their task will hear the people say, 'We did it ourselves!'

August 12th

The centipede was happy quite
Until the Toad in fun
Said, 'Pray, which leg goes after which?'
And worked her mind to such a pitch
She lay distracted in the ditch
Considering how to run.

Edmund Craster

August 13th

The Lord is compassionate and gracious,
slow to anger and abounding in love.
He will not accuse, nor will he harbour his anger for ever;

he does not treat us as our sins deserve
  or repay us according to our iniquities.
For as high as the heavens are above the earth,
  so great is his love for those who fear him;
as far as the east is from the west,
  so far has he removed our transgressions from us.
As a father has compassion on his children,
  so the Lord has compassion on those who fear him.

Psalm 103: 8 -13

August 14th

Forgive them all, O Lord:
our sins of omission and our sins of commission;
the sins of our youth and the sins of our riper years;
the sins of our souls and the sins of our bodies;
our secret and our more open sins;
our sins of ignorance and surprise,
and our more deliberate and presumptuous sin;
the sins we have done to please ourselves
and the sins we have done to please others;
the sins we know and remember,
and the sins we have forgotten;
the sins we have striven to hide from others
and the sins by which we have made others offend;
forgive them, O Lord, forgive them all for his sake,
who died for our sins and rose for our justification,
and now stands at your right hand to make intercession
for us, Jesus Christ our Lord.

John Wesley

August 15th

There is a story told of a Jewish farmer who did not get home from work before sunset one Sabbath. He had to spend the night in his field waiting for the next day's sunset so that he could return home. His rabbi chided him for his neglect and said he hoped that he had spent the time in prayer. The man replied, 'Rabbi, I am not a learned man. I cannot pray properly by myself. So I just spent the day reciting the alphabet and let God make the words of the prayers himself.'

What Language Shall They Borrow?

When angel voices sing your praises
What earthly language shall they borrow?
Will it be the tongue of the centurion,
Conquistador, or colonialist?
Or will your praise be formulated, U.N. - like,
In any of the five super - tongues
Simultaneously translated?

Or will a threadbare woman's voice,
Hidden in the gods,
Sing a solo adulation
In Gaelic, or Swahili,
Or Ki'ché?

Malcolm Ramsay

August 16th

After years of failing sight, Milton became totally blind in his forties. He asks how God can exact day labour if light is denied and then in his poem 'On His Blindness' has Patience replying:

God doth not need
Either man's work or his own gifts; who best
Bear his mild yoke, they serve him best. His state
is kingly: thousands at his bidding speed
And post o'er land and ocean without rest.
They also serve who only stand and wait.

August 17th

Lord Ashley, former Labour MP has battled for years with deafness. He once said, 'If you're deaf and you want sympathy, you'd better develop a limp.'

August 18th

Courage is fear that has said its prayers.

August 19th

George Macdonald was a 19th century Scottish congregational minister and poet, who like Milton, Francis Thompson and a great many other poets had much to say about searching and about losing and finding, or being found. The next words are from his poem Lost and Found.

I found him nearest when I missed him most;
I found him in my heart, a life in frost,
A light I knew not till my soul was dark.

George MacDonald

August 20th

For this is what the Sovereign Lord says: I myself will search for my sheep and look after them. As a shepherd looks after his scattered flock when he is with them, so will I look after my sheep.

Ezekiel 34: 11-12

I am the good shepherd; I know my sheep and my sheep know me - just as the father knows me and I know the Father - and I lay down my life for the sheep.

John 10: 14

August 21st

Lord, in our reluctance to ask for your forgiveness
and also the forgiveness of those we have hurt and maligned,
we have fallen short of your will for us.
Grant us grace to study your own forgiving spirit.
Remind us of those whom you freely forgave:
The tax-collector who took more than his fair share
but whose home you visited to bring cleansing.
The publican who could not bear to raise his head
but who prayed in humility for mercy.
The woman taken in adultery to whom your gentleness
and understanding was a balm.
The disciple who denied you and yet who accepted forgiveness -
enough to be commissioned to feed your flock.
The thief on the cross whose repentance called forth a promise of reunion in paradise.
Even those who killed you brought a plea to your lips for their forgiveness.
Lord, you did not despise the poor, nor reject those who by their sin hurt and maligned you.
Help us not to be afraid to draw close to you, the good shepherd.
Show us how to seek in your love our own forgiveness.

August 22nd

I had a wonderful experience along with other passengers travelling the sea from Fair Isle towards Cape Wrath in the North of Scotland in being able to watch a lively school of killer whales accompanying us not far from the starboard side of the ship. The excitement on board the ship was palpable.

I remember once being given a short recording of whales singing in the deep. I put this record on at an incorrect faster speed, and it could easily then be mistaken for birds' song. Their songs have identifiable themes, and if man can recognise them as such, how much more should the whales be able to.

Laurens van der Post said that whales may talk in the most tender and moving voices to one another deep down in the privacy of the sea. But they do not, even when harpooned, make any audible sound on the surface, not even in their flurry of death accompanied by the cruellest of pain.

August 23rd

An American Indian once spoke about silence and its mystery.

'The holy silence is God's voice. If you ask what are the fruits of silence, God will say: they are self-control, true courage in endurance, patience, dignity and reverence. Silence is the cornerstone of character.'

We live in an age when many are frightened of silence. There are silences to be frightened of, as for instance what Eric Lomax in 'The Railway Man' describes as one of the worst enemies of all in his Japanese prison camp - the decree of silence. He said there was an obscene aptness in the formidable silence imposed on him and his comrades, for they had only survived their previous two years in the POW camp by endless talk.

But there are silences to be cultivated to the point of love, so that we can learn to practise the presence of God even in the times when we are asked to bear the cruellest of pain. He will most surely come and join us there. He has walked the same path before us.

August 24th

Expecting him, my door was open wide:
  Then I looked round
  If any lack of service could be found.
And saw him at my side:
How entered, by what secret stair ,
I know not, knowing only he was there.

T.E. Brown

August 25th

What is more foolish, the child who is afraid of the dark, or the man afraid of the light?

Maurice Freehill

That seems like a trite remark if you have not suffered as Lomax and his fellow prisoners did in their POW camp. He said one of his colleagues, Thew, muttered under his breath once, 'I can't think of anything to think about.' Fred Smith hissed back, 'Have you thought about *everything* already?' 'Yes,' said Thew. 'Well,' said Smith, 'Start again!'

Lomax comments that after a time in captivity recycling your memories is beyond a joke, and the mind chews itself painfully over and over, cud without nutrition.

One is duly chastened when talking about silence and solitude when one hears of such harrowing experiences. Yet even when we have difficulty with silence, it is good to be quiet at the beginning of each day so that God can have the first word; and equally so at the end of the day so that God can have the last.

August 26th

Denis Thatcher was once chided for refusing to give interviews to the press. He retorted, 'Whales only get killed when they spout!'

August 27th

And he (*the Lord*) said *(to Elijah)* 'Go forth, and stand upon the mount before the Lord, and behold the Lord passed by, and a great and strong wind rent the mountains, and brake into pieces the rocks before the Lord; but the Lord was not in the wind: and after the wind an earthquake; but the Lord was not in the earthquake:

And after the earthquake a fire; but the Lord was not in the fire: and after the fire a still small voice. And it was so when Elijah heard it that he wrapped his face in his mantle, and went out and stood in the entering of the cave.

1 Kings: 19, 11-13 (AV)

August 28th

Before Prayer

I weave a silence on to my lips .... my mind .... my heart.
Calm me, O Lord, as you stilled the storm
Still me, O Lord, keep me from harm
Let all the tumult within me cease
Enfold me, O Lord, in your peace.

August 29th

Before my husband and myself had any major anxieties in our life, we were both deeply impressed by the words of the hymn 'Be Still My Soul' sung to the beautiful tune Finlandia, by Sibelius. When anxiety did come, we found much solace in the words:

Be still, my soul, thy God doth undertake
To guide the future as he hath the past,
Thy hope, thy confidence let nothing shake
All now mysterious will be bright at last
Be still, my soul: the waves and wind still know
His voice who ruled them while he dwelt below.

I was immensely touched then many years later when I heard how Christopher Reeves, the actor Superman who became totally paralysed through a riding accident, spoke of how his wife had jerked him out of his depression by saying to him, 'You are still you!' He told of how that word *'still'* came to have two meanings for him. He was still the personality he always had been, but he was also a still person, reluctantly in body, but richly in soul.

August 30th

Elizabeth I was once questioned about her impression of Christ's presence in the sacrament of holy Communion. She answered in the following lines:

> 'Twas God the word that spake it
> He took the Bread and brake it
> And what the word did make it;
> That I believe and take it.

August 31st

When Sainsbury's announced that they were becoming a bank, someone drew attention to a notice in a grocer's window in Killarney.

'The bank has decided not to sell groceries. We in turn have decided not to give credit.'

SEPTEMBER

September, dusting cobwebs from the lamps....
George MacKay Brown

September 1st

Thomas Ken, born in 1631, was a clergyman and hymn-writer known for the classics 'Awake my soul,' and 'Glory to Thee, my God this night.' He was appointed a Royal Chaplain, but lost favour when Charles II visited Winchester and Ken refused to give up his residence for Nell Gwynne, the mistress of the king. He was deprived of the bishopric of Bath and Wells in 1691 as he had refused to take the oath of allegiance to William III. He could refuse the associates of royalty house-room, and in writing this prayer for hospitality, speaks of the 'rough threshold' that is sometimes necessary.

O God
Make the door of this house wide enough
to receive all who need human love and fellowship,
and a Heavenly Father's care.
Make it narrow enough
to shut out all envy, pride and hate.
Make its threshold smooth enough
to be no stumbling block to children
or to straying feet.
But make it rough enough
to turn back the tempter's power.
Make it a gateway to your eternal kingdom.

Thomas Ken

September 2nd

Michel Quoist in Pathways To Prayer talks about the difficulty of forgetting things in the past that would be best forgotten. He says we try to be brave and turn over a page of memory quickly so that we do not see it, but wherever there is a breath of wind, the photo album of our old memories opens up again.

September 3rd

All happy families resemble each other but each unhappy family is unhappy in its own way.

Leo Tolstoy (Anna Karenina)

September 4th

I was very young - still at primary school - when for some reason or other my attention was drawn to a poem which would now be unfamiliar to most youngsters. I remember, however, committing it to heart, and when a young friend came to my home to play at 'houses' with our various dolls as guests, I quoted the poem to her. I can still see our humble kitchen with its plain furniture, the fire in the grate, and my friend's rather bewildered expression as I recited the poem to her. It must have sounded so priggish that she could well have been put off poetry for life. Yet I still love the poem.

Preparations

Yet, if His Majesty, our Sovereign Lord,
Should of his own accord
Friendly himself invite,
And say, 'I'll be your guest tomorrow night,'
How should we stir ourselves, call and command
All hands to work! 'Let no man idle stand!

'Set me fine Spanish tables in the hall;
See they be fitted all;
Let there be room to eat
And order taken that there want no meat.
See every sconce and candlestick made bright,
That without tapers they may give a light.

'Look to the presence; are the carpets spread,
The dazie o'er the head,
The cushions in the chairs,
And all the candles lighted on the stairs?
Perfume the chambers, and in any case
Let each man give attendance in his place!'

Thus if the king were coming would we do;
And 'twere good reason too;
For 'tis a duteous thing to do
To show all honour to an earthly king,
And after all our travail and our cost,
So he be pleased, to think no labour lost.

But at the coming of the King of Heaven
All's set at six and seven;
We wallow in our sin,
Christ cannot find a chamber in the inn.
We entertain Him always like a stranger,
And as at first, still lodge Him in the manger.

17th century anon

September 5th

Francis Quarles once said that the heart is a small thing, but desireth great matters. It is not sufficient for a kite's dinner, yet the whole world is not sufficient for it. And Dietrich Bonhoeffer once said that in the Biblical sense the heart is more than just the inward man; it is the whole man in relation to God.

September 6th

For this reason I kneel before the Father, from whom his whole family in heaven and on earth derives its name. I pray that out of his glorious riches he may strengthen you with power through his spirit in your inner being, so that Christ may dwell in your hearts through faith. And I pray that you, being rooted and grounded in love, may have power, together with all the saints, to grasp how wide and long and high and deep is the love of Christ, and to know this love that surpasses knowledge - that you may be filled to the measure of all the fulness of God.
Now to him that is able to do immeasurably more than all we ask or imagine, according to his power that is at work within us, to him be glory in the church and in Christ Jesus throughout all generations, for ever and ever, Amen.

Ephesians 3: 14-21

September 7th

Bless our home, Father,
that we cherish the bread before there is none
discover each other before we leave,
and enjoy each other for what we are
while we have time

Hawaiian Prayer

September 8th

I went to live in a new area and found most folk very hospitable, but especially a couple whose home always, whatever their own circumstances, had an open door and a welcoming table.

When I was leaving the area I told them how impressed I had been by their natural warmth.

The husband told me a touching story. He said he was nine before he realised home should be like that. Though his own was upright, he had never been encouraged on any occasion to bring his mates home. One day one of those mates asked him to go with him on his school bus, as he was invited for tea. As they got off the bus near his friend's house, he saw two figures by the gate with arms outstretched to greet them both with a hug and a welcome. He told me that there and then he resolved when he had his own home its door would be an ever-open door to all comers, and it would have a welcoming table for all guests. I was reminded of this other Hawaiian Blessing:

> Father of all mankind
> Make the roof of my house wide enough for all opinions
> Oil the door of my house so it opens easily to friend and stranger
> And set such a table in my house
> That my whole family may speak freely and kindly around it.

September 9th

Isaac Newton was once found putting a horseshoe over his front door, and saying, 'That's for luck!' A friend said, 'But I thought you always said you were not superstitious.'

'I'm not,' retorted Newton, 'but they tell me it works anyway!'

September 10th

> Lord of all pots and pans and things
> Since I've no time to be
> A saint by doing lovely things
> Or watching late with Thee
> Or dreaming in the dawn light
> Or storming heaven's gates,
> Make me a saint by getting meals
> And washing up the plates.

Fay Inchfawn

September 11th

The time of business does not differ from the time of prayer, and in the noise and clutter of my kitchen, while several persons are at the same time calling for different things, I possess God in as great tranquillity as if I were on my knees at the Blessed Sacrament.

Brother Lawrence

September 12th

Lloyd George found brokering peace with Irish Republicans in his day just as exasperating as it often is today. He said of De Valera when he was Taoiseach of Eire, that negotiating with him was just like trying to pick up mercury with a fork.

De Valera replied, 'Why doesn't he just use a spoon?'

September 13th

What after all is Apollos? And what is Paul? Only servants, through whom you came to believe - as the Lord has assigned to each his task. I planted the seed, Apollos watered it, but God made it grow. So neither he who plants nor he who waters is anything, but only God who makes things grow. The man who plants and the man who waters have one purpose, and each will be rewarded according to his own labour. For we are God's fellow-workers, you are God's field, God's building.

By the grace God has given me, I laid a foundation as an expert builder, and someone else is building on it. But each one should be careful how he builds. For no-one can lay any other foundation other than the one already laid, which is Christ Jesus.

1 Corinthians 3: 5-11

September 14th

Teach me, my God and King
In all things thee to see
And what I do in anything,
To do it as for thee!

A servant with this clause
Makes drudgery divine
Who sweeps a room as for thy laws
Makes that and the action fine.

George Herbert

September 15th

I have just been reading in a local paper about an unusual find on an Angus beach of dozens of starfish which for some unknown reason had been washed above the water line, some stranded on pebbles and some in shallow rock pools. This reminded me of what someone had told me about walking along a South American beach where not dozens, but hundreds of starfish were lying stranded above the water line. A woman was lifting them one by one and hurling them back out to sea. A passer-by said to her, 'What you're doing won't make any difference.' She opened her hand and revealed the starfish she was about to return to the ocean, and replied, 'It will certainly make a lot of difference to this one.'

Edward Pusey once said: Nothing is too little to be ordered by our Father; nothing too little in which to see his hand; nothing, which touches our souls, too little to accept from him; nothing too little to be done to him.

September 16th

A drip once said to the ocean,
I have a notion
That I am really the ocean
The only difference I can see
Is just a matter of degree

Hans Hesse

September 17th

Julian Bream, the classical guitarist, was driving his MG car in 1984 with his right arm hanging over the door, when he smashed it against a railway parapet. He describes the accident as an interesting moment in his life, for both his elbow and his forearm were broken. He was told that it would be unlikely he would play his guitar successfully again. But he was back within months stating that his now foreshortened arm worked even more beautifully when he laid it on the guitar. From stumbling blocks to stepping stones !

September 18th

Some want to work within the sound
Of chapel or of bell
I want to run a rescue shop
Within a yard of hell.

C.T. Studd

September 19th

The work of a Beethoven, and the work of a charwoman, become spiritual on precisely the same condition, that of being offered to God, of being done humbly, 'as to the Lord.' This does not mean, of course, that it is for anyone a mere toss-up whether he should sweep rooms or compose symphonies. A mole must dig to the glory of God, and a cock must crow.

C.S. Lewis

September 20th

Two are better than one
  Because they have a good return for their work:
If one falls down,
  his friend can help him up.
But pity the man who falls
  and has no-one to help him up!
Also, if two lie down together, they will keep warm,
But how can one keep warm alone?
Though one may be overpowered,
  two can defend themselves.
A cord of three strands is not easily broken.

Ecclesiastes 4: 9-12

September 21st

O happy home, where thou art loved the dearest,
Thou loving friend and Saviour of our race
And where among the guests there never cometh
One who can hold such high and honoured place!

O happy home, where each one serves thee, lowly,
Whatever his appointed work may be,
Till every common task seems great and holy,
When it is done, O Lord, as unto thee!

O happy home, where thou art not forgotten
When joy is overflowing, full and free:
O happy home, where every wounded spirit
Is brought, Physician, Comforter, to thee.

Until at last, when earth's day's work is ended
All meet thee in the blessed home above
From whence thou camest, where thou hast ascended,
Thy everlasting home of peace and love.

Karl J.B. Spitta - Tr. S.L. Findlater

September 22nd

I had the great privilege some time back of visiting at her home in Paateri, in Karelia, Finland the sculptress Eva Ryynänen. In the grounds of her home, amongst other sculptures, she had built a little chapel and every pew she had carved out of a trunk of a tree. The chapel as well as her home contained many beautiful works of art. She was a tiny little person, and though she and her husband were in their eighties, he was still her assistant helping her with the heavy job of all the mechanics necessary in working with large tree trunks. Much earlier in life he gave up farming, as he saw the quality of her work develop and knew the potential. Eva herself had been brought up on a farm, where her father worked in the evenings mending sleighs and harnesses. At a very early age she picked up the left-over bits of wood from the floor and spent her time carving them into sparrows, chaffinches and the like, even at that early age carving a little horse which fitted into a match box.

Eva in describing her love of working with wood, said that she makes friends with a piece of wood, looks at it and touches it until she realises what image is within it. Only then does she go to work.

I have a great admiration for those who have developed that wonderful insight and patience, and it always draws me to think of our own Creator who even in the most unlikely and unloveable human beings that we may be, makes friends with us, looks lovingly upon us and realises how we can be changed into something worthwhile and even beautiful. It is hard to be like him in this respect for we so often shun the unlovely, the difficult, the twisted, the forlorn.

September 23rd

Action without vision is pointless. Vision without action is fruitless. But action and vision together can change the world.

September 24th

What crazy existence is this we've had
  That so undermined us?
We have kept pace with progress and rushed straight ahead
  And left ourselves behind us.

Karl Fraus

September 25th

Hammond Innes was a prolific writer of adventure stories. He developed a passion for forestry and he planted about two million trees in Suffolk, Wales and Australia. He said that he had done this to atone for all those that had been pulped up to produce his thrillers. 'Books,' he used to say, 'are nothing but trees with squiggles on them.'

September 26th

Writers and musicians, and indeed artists of all categories, can be notoriously ungenerous to each other when assessing achievement. Max Bruch once played a new composition of his for Brahms to assess. Brahms' only comment was, 'Do tell me where you buy your manuscript paper. It's first class!'

September 27th

This is what the Lord says;

'Let not the wise man boast of his wisdom
or the strong man boast of his strength
or the rich man boast of his riches,
but let him that boasts boast about this;
that he understands and knows me,
that I am the Lord, who exercises kindness,
justice and righteousness on earth,
for in these I delight'
declares the Lord.

Jeremiah 9: 23-24

September 28th

O Thou, who camest from above
The pure celestial fire to impart
Kindle a flame of sacred love
On the mean altar of my heart.

Then let it for thy glory burn
With inextinguishable blaze
And trembling to its source return
In humble prayer and fervent praise.

Jesus, confirm my heart's desire
To work and speak and think for thee
Still let me guard the holy fire
And still stir up thy gift in me.

Ready for all thy perfect will
My acts of faith and love repeat
Till death thy endless mercies seal
And make the sacrifice complete.

Charles Wesley

September 29th

Leo Szilard, a scientist, started keeping a diary which he said was not for publication, but to keep a record of the facts for God.

One of his friends said, 'Maybe God already knows the facts.'

Szilard replied, 'Ah, but he doesn't know this version of the facts!'

Children sometimes have a quaint idea of what information needs to be given to God. One youngster known to me was reminded at bedtime that she had been very naughty and should tell God about it. But she sturdily replied, 'God is far too busy to be bothered with little things like that!' One of my own youngsters did not consider God too busy to deal with matters which concerned her, for she prayed that God would bless 'poor old Michael Finnegan, for he had whiskers on his chinnegan and the wind came out and blew them in again!'

September 30th

Sir Arthur Conan Doyle, the Edinburgh doctor who became famous for his Sherlock Holmes tales, became a spiritualist later in life. He is not so well-known as a poet, but I have always enjoyed this piece about a pugilist preacher who used the powers he knew best when trying to proclaim the Gospel.

Pride Of Nottingham

You didn't know of Bendigo! Well, that knocks me out!
Who's your board school teacher? What's he been about?
Chock-a-block with fairy tales, full of useless cram,
And never heard of Bendigo, the pride of Nottingham.

Bendy, he turned Methodist - he said he felt a call,
He stumped the country preachin' and you bet he filled the hall,
If you seed him in the pulpit, a bleatin' like a lamb,
You'd never know bold Bendigo, the pride of Nottingham!

His hat was like a funeral, he'd got a waiter's coat,
With a hallelujah collar and a choker round his throat
His pals would laugh and say in chaff that Bendigo was right
In takin' on the devil, since he'd no-one else to fight.

But he was very earnest, improvin' day by day,
A-workin' and a-preachin' just as his duty lay;
But the devil he was waitin', and in the final bout
He hit him hard below his guard and knocked poor Bendy out.

Now I'll tell you how it happened. He was preachin' down in
    Brum,
He was billed just like a circus - you should see the people come,
The chapel it was crowded out, and in the foremost row
There were half a dozen bruisers who'd a grudge at Bendigo.

There was Tommy Platt of Bradford, Solly Jones of Perry Bar,
Long Connor from the Bull Ring, the same wot drew with Carr,
Jack Ball the fightin' gunsmith, Joe Murphy from the News,
And Iky Moss the bettin' boss, the Champion of the Jews.

A very pretty handful a-sittin' in a string,
Full of beer and impudence, ripe for anything,
Sittin' in a string there, right under Bendy's nose,
If his message was for sinners, he would make a start on those.

Soon he had them chaffin': 'Hi, Bendy! here's a go!'
'How much are you coppin' from this Jump-to-Glory show?'
'Stow it Bendy! Left the ring! Mighty spry of you!
Didn't everybody know the Ring was leavin' you?'

Bendy fairly sweated as he stood above and prayed,
'Look down, O Lord, and grip me in a stranglehold!' he said.
'Fix me with a stranglehold! Put a stop on me!
I'm slippin', Lord, I'm slippin' and I'm clingin' hard to Thee!'

But the roughs they kept on chaffin' and the uproar it was such
That the preacher in the pulpit might be talkin' double Dutch,
Till a workin' man he shouted, a-jumpin' to his feet,
'Give us a lead, your reverence, and heave 'em in the street.'

Then Bendy said, 'Good Lord, since first I left my sinful ways,
Thou knowest that to Thee alone I've given all my days,
But now, dear Lord' (and here he left his Bible on the shelf)
'I'll take with your permission just five minutes for myself.'

He vaulted from the pulpit like a tiger from his den,
They say it was a lovely sight to see him floor his men;
Right and left and left and right, straight and true and hard,
Till the Ebenezer Chapel was just like a knacker's yard.

Platt was standin' on his back, and lookin' at his toes,
Solly Jones of Perry Bar was feelin' for his nose,
Connor of the Bull Ring had all that he could do
Rakin' for his ivories that lay about the pew.

Jack Ball the fightin' gunsmith was in a peaceful sleep,
Joe Murphy lay across him, all tied up in a heap,
Five of them was twisted in a tangle on the floor,
And Iky Moss, the bettin' boss, had sprinted for the door.

Five repentant fightin' men, sittin' in a row,
Listenin' to words of grace from Mister Bendigo,
Listenin' to his reverence, all as good as gold,
Pretty little baa-lambs, gathered to the fold.

So that's the way that Bendy ran his mission in the slum,
And preached the holy Gospel to the fightin' men of Brum,
'The Lord' (said he) 'has given me a message from on high,
And if you interrupt Him I will know the reason why!'

But to think of all your schoolin', clean wasted, thrown away,
Darned if I can make out what you're learnin' all the day,
Grubbin' up old fairy tales, fillin' up with cram,
And didn't know of Bendigo, the pride of Nottingham.

OCTOBER

Earth is crammed with Heaven
And every common bush afire with God
Elizabeth Barrett Browning

October 1st

In the Jewish tradition, Yom Kippur, or the Day of Atonement is usually celebrated on October 10th, based on the statutes of Leviticus 16: 29-34. The following prayer is a Yom Kippur Prayer taken from Parabola Magazine, New York.

Like the clay in the hand of the potter
Who thickens or thins it at his will,
So we are in Thy hand, gracious God,
Forgive our sin, Thy covenant fulfil

Like a stone in the hands of the mason
Who preserves or breaks it at his will
So we are in Thy hand, Lord of life,
Forgive our sin, Thy covenant fulfil

Like iron in the hand of the craftsman
Who forges or cools it at his will,
We are in Thy hand, our Keeper
Forgive our sin, Thy covenant fulfil.

Like the wheel in the hand of the seaman
Who directs or holds it at his will,
So are we in Thy hand, loving God,
Forgive our sin, Thy covenant fulfil.

Like the glass in the hand of the blower
Who dissolves or shapes it at his will,
So are we in Thy hand, God of grace
Forgive our sin, Thy covenant fulfil.

Like the cloth in the hand of the tailor
Who smoothens or drapes it at his will,
So are we in Thy hand, righteous God,
Forgive our sin, Thy covenant fulfil.

Like silver in the hand of the smelter
Who refines or blends it at his will,
So are we in Thy hand, our Healer,
Forgive our sin, Thy covenant fulfil.

October 2nd

Life is not hurrying on to a receding future
nor hankering after an imagined past
It is the turning aside like Moses
to the miracle of the lit bush
to a brightness that seemed
as transitory as your youth once
but is the eternity that awaits you.

R.S. Thomas

October 3rd

This very remarkable man
Commends a most practical plan:
You can do what you want
If you don't think you can't
So don't think you can't - THINK YOU CAN!

October 4th

When the Chief Rabbi, Jonathan Sacks was asked how he spent his time when relaxing he said that he had several strategies - the best being to get his kids to give him a big hug! He said music helped as well. When asked if he ever gave way to despair, he said, 'Never! If I ever get close to it I read the Bible and I remember that Moses had it worse!'

October 5th

Once when Samuel Beckett was at a rehearsal of one of his plays at the Royal Court, one of the actors, being over-awed by the author's presence, gave up, crying, 'I'm failing!'

Beckett tried to encourage him. 'Just go on failing. Go on. Only next time try to fail better!'

October 6th

If the axe is dull
and the edge unsharpened
more strength is needed
but skill will bring success.

Ecclesiastes 10: 10

Now my son, the Lord be with you, and may you have success and build the house of the Lord your God, as he said you would. May the Lord give you discretion and understanding......Then you will have success if you are careful to observe the decrees and the laws that the Lord gave to Moses for Israel. Be strong and courageous. Do not be afraid or discouraged.

1 Chronicles 22: 11-13

October 7th

LORD IT IS NIGHT

The night is for stillness
Let us be still in the presence of God.

It is night after a long day.
What has been done has been done;
What has not been done has not been done.
Let it be.

The night is dark.
Let our fears of the darkness of the world
and of our own lives
rest in you.

The night is quiet.
Let the quietness of your peace enfold us,
all dear to us,
and all who have no peace.

The night heralds the dawn.
Let us look expectantly to a new day,
new joys, new possibilities.
In your name we pray. Amen

A Maori Prayer

October 8th

Diogenes was the best known of the Greek philosophers called Cynics. He was reputed to live in a wine barrel, or rather in a series of barrels - all empty! His only possessions were a clock, a stick and a bread bag, for the Cynics of that day taught that happiness was not to be found in material luxury or power or even good health. Diogenes was visited by Alexander the Great who asked him if there was anything he could do for him.

Diogenes replied, 'Stand to one side. You are blocking the sun!'

October 9th

Ralph Waldo Emerson once said that most of the shadows in our lives are caused by standing in the way of our own sunshine.

October 10th

> He drew a circle that shut me out
> Heretic, rebel, a thing to flout
> But Love and I had the wit to win
> We drew a circle that shut him in.

October 11th

Voltaire was asked on his deathbed to renounce the devil. 'Ah no,' he replied, 'This is no time to make enemies!'

October 12th

Euphemisms exist in all languages for death. In English we glibly talk about 'kicking the bucket,' 'popping your clogs,' or 'snuffing the candle.' In French I believe they say, 'fermer son parapluie' or 'fold up your umbrella.' They also say, 'plus mal aux dents,' or 'have no more toothache.' I like the French euphemisms better, for they both imply leaving behind trouble of one kind or another.

The Scriptures have no inhibitions. They speak quite clearly and quite often about death. If you look at any concordance you will be overwhelmed by references. But the wonderful thing is that like the French euphemisms, so many of the Scriptural references are full of hope and anticipation of a better life to come, with very definite assurances which should make the use of the word death acceptable, instead of searching for a euphemism to cover our human fear of it.

October 13th

Since then, you have been raised with Christ, set your hearts on things above, where Christ is seated at the right hand of God. Set your minds on things above, not on earthly things. For you died, and your life is now hidden with Christ in God. When Christ, who is your life, appears then will you also appear with him in glory.

Colossians 3: 1-4

October 14th

Holy Spirit, come among us
and help us to proclaim
the freedom of God's children
the glory of Christ's name.

As the seed that once was scattered
becomes our daily bread,
so may your church be gathered
transformed to faith from dread.

Have pity on our sorrows
bring healing to our pain
and make us one with all the poor
that they may hope again.

As the life that once was crossed out
became our daily breath
so may your church rejoicing
live the life that conquers death.

Michael Urch

October 15th

If you think living life in a barrel like Diogenes is strange, then what about some early Christians who were nicknamed Stylites. A 'stylite' was a pillar dweller. The first such was St. Simeon, the Stylite who lived in the 5th century. He was a Syrian and had spent nine years in a monastery there without ever leaving his cell. Then he appeared near Antioch where he established himself in a pillar, 72 feet high, and from there he preached twice a day to all who would listen. Others followed his example including one called Daniel, who took over his pillar when Simeon died.

I have met some modern eccentrics, who seem to think they work best if they erect some strange high platform from which to thunder at their hearers. One such operated in a square at Christchurch, New Zealand, where he used a ladder to ascend to his platform. More than once I saw the crowds of young and old who came not only to listen but to rant back. I never ever found out if anyone was ever really challenged or influenced by his harangue, or whether he was just regarded as a curiosity.

In my youth, I remember a minister, who in the old-fashioned style was safely shut into his pulpit each Sunday, before he started the arm-flailing and the loud lambasting of his congregation, all, as he used to declare regularly, he believed were hell-ward bound. One child, brought into such proceedings for the first time, quivered and shook and then asked her mother anxiously, 'What will we all do if he escapes?'

We have travelled far from those days, and each age has its drawbacks. I worry today when I consider the celebrity cult. I get the impression that those in charge of religious affairs, including the media, are trawling the country to find what celebrities will help them entertain the masses, rather than revealing the truths of Christianity and the person of Christ to them. There does seem a dearth of good old-fashioned conviction sometimes.

If we feel we have to raise a platform to proclaim our views, it should be to elevate the Christ, and him alone.

October 16th

'The celebrity is a person who is well-known for his well-knownness.'

Daniel J. Boorsten

'It must be unnerving to be so famous that you know they are going to come in the moment you croak . . . and treat everything you say with reverence.'

Bill Bryson

October 17th

It fortifies my soul to know
That, though I perish, Truth is so
That howsoe'er I stray and range
Whate'er I do, Thou dost not change.
I steadier step when I recall
That if I slip, Thou dost not fall.

A.H. Clough

October 18th

James MacNeill Whistler, the famous artist, failed his exams for the army, afterwards saying that if silicone had been a gas, he would have passed and might have become a major-general, instead of a painter.

A pupil was preparing for a different set of exams. She told her mathematics teacher she was praying to God that she would pass. Her maths mistress gave her the gentle suggestion that she should appeal to St. Jude instead, since he was the saint of 'hopeless cases.'

October 19th

T.S. Eliot has said we are given brief moments of fusion with God which transform us, but they are only moments.

> ....and the rest
> Is prayer, observance, discipline, thought and action.

October 20th

Finally, be strong in the Lord and in his mighty power. Put on the full armour of God so that you can take your stand against the devil's schemes. For our struggle is not against flesh and blood, but against the rulers, against the authorities, and against the spiritual forces of evil in the heavenly realms. Therefore put on the whole armour of God, so that when the day of evil comes, you may be able to stand your ground, and after you have done everything to stand.

Stand firm then, with the belt of truth buckled round your waist, with the breastplate of righteousness in place, and your feet fitted with the readiness that comes from the gospel of peace. In addition to all this, take up the shield of faith, with which you can extinguish all the flaming arrows of the evil one. Take the helmet of salvation and the sword of the Spirit, which is the word of God.

Ephesians 6: 10-17

October 21st

> I ask no dream, no prophet - ecstasies
> No sudden rending of the veil of clay
> No angel - visitant, no opening skies;
> But take the dimness of my soul away.
> Teach me to feel that thou art always nigh
> Teach me the struggles of the soul to bear
> To check the rising doubt, the rebel sigh;
> Teach me the patience of unanswered prayer.

George Croly

October 22nd

In Helsinki as far back as 1906, the Square Temppeliaukio was so named with the idea that a church would be built there. An architectural competition was instituted, but proceedings were interrupted by the Second World War. It was 1961 before the plans for the now famous Rock Church by two architect brothers, Timo and Tuomo Suomalainen, won the competition, and work began.

The basic idea was to preserve the rock formation in the Square, so the essential construction has been formed by going as deeply as possible into the natural stone. The inner walls are of bedrock and quarried stone, and this has been left rough, both for artistic and aesthetic purposes. Water runs down the walls from the rock face and is drained away through the floor. The altar wall is formed from an ice-age rock crevice, and in the usually wonderful Finnish summer, during the morning service, the sunlight falls across the altar. The altar table is a slab of granite and there is a crucifix portraying Christ both as sufferer and victor.

The words we are asked to ponder in this unique and beautiful church are these:

> Rejoice at the beauty of this house of God
> Respect its sanctity
> Your Creator and Redeemer is near
> Peace be with you.

October 23rd

> Rock of ages, cleft for me
> Let me hide myself in thee;
> Let the water and the blood
> From thy riven side which flowed,
> Be of sin the double cure
> Cleanse me from its guilt and power.

Augustus M. Toplady

October 24th

There are countless places of refuge, there is only one place of salvation; but the possibilities of salvation again, are as numerous as all the places of refuge.

Franz Kafka

October 25th

> Nothing is wasted, nothing is in vain;
> The seas roll over, but the rocks remain.

A.P. Herbert

NOVEMBER

The frost performs its secret ministry
Unhelped by any wind
Samuel Taylor Coleridge

November 1st

On November 14th, 1940 Coventry Cathedral was destroyed in an air raid, and later in Dresden there was similar devastation. A new cathedral was consecrated in Coventry in 1962 and this became a place of reconciliation. For me the most lasting impression is of the part in the old ruins where the altar has a cross of nails and a cross of charred wood. A prayer was composed in 1964 for the International Students' Festival and each day at lunch time this prayer is prayed in the chapel of reconciliation.

Father forgive
The hatred which divides nation from nation
race from race, class from class.
Father forgive
the greed which exploits the labours of men
and lays waste the earth.
Father forgive
our envy of the welfare and happiness of others.
Father forgive
our indifference to the plight of the homeless and the refugee.
Father forgive
the lust which uses for ignoble ends the bodies of men and women
Father forgive
The pride which leads to trust in ourselves and not in God.
Father forgive.

November 2nd

The seven deadly or cardinal sins are pride, lechery, envy, anger, covetousness, gluttony and sloth. When a Roman Catholic priest called Sin was given his hat when he became Cardinal of the Philippines, he said, 'Everyone will now have to be told that there is an eighth cardinal sin.'

November 3rd

I have always had to wrestle with something that C.S.Lewis once said: that forgiving someone not seven times, but seventy times seven as Peter was told, might very well mean not just having to forgive four hundred and ninety sins, but having to forgive the same sin four hundred and ninety times. I am always reminded when I think of that how one of my youngsters disobeyed me and I sent her to her room to think over her misdeed. She was very offended and said, 'You only told me once not to do that. Usually I can wait until you have said, "I'm telling you this for the *last* time."'

There is something called 'tough love' and we do not always practise it, because forgiveness does not just mean turning a blind eye to our own wrong-doings, or the wrong-doings of others. Redress may be required. True reconciliation may be required as well as genuine repentance.

Mental health is often the outcome of right relationships, and right relationships involve repentance and forgiveness.

It is a sublime, Christlike privilege to forgive, just as it is to be forgiven.

November 4th

The quality of mercy is not strained,
It droppeth as the gentle rain from heaven
Upon the place beneath: it is twice blessed;
It blesseth him that gives and him that takes:
'Tis mightiest in the mightiest ......

It is an attribute to God himself,
And earthly power doth then show likest God's
When mercy seasons justice.

Shakespeare (Merchant of Venice)

November 5th

There are some people who are very resourceful
At being remorseful,
And who apparently feel that the best way to make friends
Is to do something terrible and then make amends.

Ogden Nash

November 6th

This is the message we have heard from him and have declared to you: God is light; in him there is no darkness at all. If we claim

to have fellowship with him yet walk in the darkness, we lie and live not by the truth. But if we walk in the light as he is in the light, we have fellowship with one another, and the blood of Jesus, his Son, purifies us from all sin.
If we claim to be without sin, we deceive ourselves and the truth is not in us. If we confess our sins, he is faithful and just to forgive us our sins and purify us from all unrighteousness. If we claim we have not sinned, we make him out to be a liar and his word has no place in our lives.

1 John 1: 5-10

November 7th

The following prayer was composed by John Donne, Dean of St. Paul's, when he was seriously ill in 1623. According to Isaac Walton he had it set to a most grave and solemn tune, which he often asked to be sung, especially by St. Paul's Choristers at evening services.

Wilt thou forgive that sin where I begun,
Which is my sin, though it were done before?
Wilt thou forgive those sins through which I run,
And do them still, though still I do deplore?
When thou hast done, thou hast not done,
  For I have more.

Wilt thou forgive that sin by which I won
Others to sin? and made my sin their door?
Wilt thou forgive that sin which I did shun
A year or two but wallowed in a score?
When thou hast done, thou hast not done,
  for I have more.

I have a sin of fear, that when I have spun
My last thread, I shall perish on the shore;
Swear by thyself, that at my death thy Son
Shall shine as he shines now, and heretofore;
And having done that thou hast done,
  I have no more.

November 8th

G.A. Studdert-Kennedy was a First World War Chaplain and a poet and writer. He tells how in the summer of 1917 he was running through a wooded copse under heavy shelling when he stumbled and fell over something. He found lying there an undersized, underfed German boy with a wound in his stomach and a hole in his head. He muttered to himself, 'You poor little devil, what had you got to do with it? There's not much of the great blonde Prussian about you!' Then, said Studdert-Kennedy, there came light. 'It may have been pure imagination, but that does not mean it was not reality, for what is called imagination is often the road to reality. It seemed to me that the boy disappeared and in his place there lay the Christ upon his cross, and cried, "Inasmuch as ye have done it unto the least of these my little ones ye have done it unto me." From that moment on I never saw a battlefield as anything but a crucifix. From that moment on I never saw the world as anything but a crucifix.'

November 9th

One day it is going to dawn on the human race that war is as barbaric a means of resolving conflict as cannibalism is as a means of coping with diet deficiencies.

Bruce Kent

Then shall all shackles fall; the stormy clangour
Of wild war-music o'er the earth shall cease
Love shall tread out the baleful fire of anger
And in its ashes plant the tree of peace

John Greenleaf Whittier

November 10th

A pupil was answering questions in his History examination. 'The Armistice was signed after the First World War. Since then there has been two minutes' peace each year.'

November 11th

On this Remembrance Day, many will have their own personal thoughts and prayers and tears. Perhaps the words of Major Malcolm Boyle will be a solace to some. He was killed in action just after the D-Day landings in 1944 and this poem was found in his Bible later.

If I should never see the moon again
Rising red-gold across the harvest field,
Or feel the stinging of soft, April rain
As the brown earth her hidden treasures yield

If I should never taste the salt sea spray
As the ship beats her course against the breeze,
Or smell the dog-rose and the new-mown hay,
Or moss or primrose underneath the trees

If I should never hear the thrushes wake
Long before sunrise in the glimmering dawn,
Or watch the huge Atlantic rollers break
Against the rugged cliffs in baffling scorn

If I have said good-bye to stream and wood
To the wide ocean and the green-clad hill,
I know that he who made that world so good
Has somewhere made a heaven better still.

Then I bear witness with my latest breath
Knowing the Love of God
I fear not death.

November 12th

Bring us, O Lord God, at our last awakening, into the house and gate of heaven, to enter into that gate and dwell in that house, where there shall be no darkness nor dazzling, but one equal light; no noise nor silence, but one equal music; no fears nor hopes, but one equal possession; no ends nor beginnings, but one equal eternity; in the habitations of Thy glory and dominion, world without end.

John Donne

November 13th

I know that my Redeemer lives,
    and that in the end he will stand upon the earth.
And after my skin has been destroyed,
    yet in my flesh I will see God;
I myself will see him
    with my own eyes - I, and not another.
How my heart yearns within me!

Job 19: 25-27

November 14th

PRAYER FOR THE SORROWING

Lord God of compassion
whose heart is the heart of Jesus our brother
whose love enfolds all your children:

Let our waiting
be a waiting in hope and peace,
for no-one is lost to you.

Let us not fear to offer you
our sorrow with our praise
for you have made our pain your own.

Let us find joy in holy memories
and give you thanks
for they promise the joy of your kingdom.

Let us bring freely before you
our shadows and our regrets
for you always forgive and heal.

Let us wait with a quiet heart
for Christ to whom all are dear
for he has made his home in our midst.

Let us trust that Christ will come
to make us one with all the saints
for his Spirit is ever with us.

All praise to you, our Father
to your son, Jesus Christ, our Lord
to the Spirit of comfort and light
both now and forever, Amen

Michael Urch

November 15th

One of the most moving stories I have ever read was told by John V. Taylor in his book 'The Go-Between God.' A West Indian woman had been given the terrible news that her husband had been killed in a road accident, and no matter who came to try to give her comfort, she remained uncommunicative, sitting stunned, unweeping, seemingly in a trance. Then a teacher of her children came in, and without a word just put her arm around the hard unyielding shoulders, and clasped the grieving woman tightly. As the unrelenting pain seeped through, the teacher's tears silently began to flow, falling on the two hands linked in the woman's lap.

Nothing happened other than that for a while, until at last the West Indian woman began to sob and her tears mingled with those of the still silent teacher. Not a word was spoken and later the teacher slipped quietly away.

John V. Taylor says, 'That is the embrace of God, his kiss of life. That is the embrace of his mission and of our intercession. And the Holy Spirit is the straining muscles of an arm, the film of sweat between pressed cheeks, the mingled wetness on the back of clasped hands. He is as close and unobtrusive as that and as irresistibly strong.'

It is good to remember that when we are lost for words, there is the precious ministry of presence - just being there for someone.

November 16th

When Christians say the Christ-life is in them, they do not mean something mental or moral. When they speak of being 'in Christ' or of Christ being 'in them,' this is not simply a way of saying that they are thinking about Christ or copying him. They mean that Christ is actually operating through them; that the whole mass of Christians are the physical organism through which Christ acts - that we are his fingers and muscles, the cells of his body.

C.S. Lewis

November 17th

A Chasidic Saying: One should not make a great to-do about serving God. Does the hand boast when it carries out what the heart wills?

November 18th

Les Murray, the Australian poet, won the T.S.Eliot prize in 1997. He had converted from Free Presbyterianism to Catholicism earlier. Someone asked him how he could reconcile things like Auschwitz with a loving God. He said, 'God sees both sides of death. We only see one side of it.'

This reminds me of a game I watched my two young daughters

play with a couple of visitors. They spread out a sheet of paper on the floor and asked them both to stand on it without touching each other. After various contortions the visitors declared it impossible. Then my two little girls took the sheet of paper and slid it under the door with half on each side. They shut the door firmly over it but with one on the outside and one on the inside. The door between prevented tangible communication.

As I watched this little game in progress, it seemed that a new parable had been enacted. There is a door called death which separates us from those in Christ's presence. Yet our lives and theirs are not severed. The communion of saints is a wonderfully reassuring doctrine.

Death hides, but it does not divide
Thou art but on Christ's other side;
Thou art with Christ and Christ with me.
In him I still am close to thee.

November 19th

The cry of man's anguish went up to God,
'Lord, take away pain,
The shadow that darkens the world thou hast made
The close, coiling chain
That strangles the heart; the burden that weighs
On the wings that would soar -
Lord, take away pain from the world thou hast made
That it love thee the more!'

Then answered the Lord to the cry of the world,
'Shall I take away pain,
And with it the power of the soul to endure,
Made strong by the strain?
Shall I take away pity that knits heart to heart,
And sacrifice high?
Will ye lose all your heroes that lift from the fire
White brows to the sky?

'Shall I take away love that redeems with a price
And smiles with its loss?
Can you spare from your lives that would cling on to mine
The Christ on his cross?'

Anonymous

November 20th

Surely he hath borne our griefs, and carried our sorrows: yet we did esteem him stricken, smitten of God and afflicted.
But he was wounded for our transgressions, he was bruised for our iniquities: the chastisement of our peace was upon him; and with his stripes we are healed.
All we like sheep have gone astray; we have turned everyone to his own way; and the Lord hath laid on him the iniquity of us all.

Isaiah 53: 4-6 (AV)

November 21st

O God of love, we pray you to give us love:
Love in our thinking, love in our speaking,
Love in our doing,
And love in the hidden places of our souls;
Love of our neighbours near and far;
Love of our friends old and new;
Love of those with whom we find it hard to bear,
And love of those who find it hard to bear with us;
Love of those with whom we work,
And love of those with whom we take our ease;
Love in joy, love in sorrow;
Love in life and love in death;
That so at length we may be worthy to dwell with you
Who are eternal love.

Archbishop William Temple

November 22nd

There is a huge boulder called Arthur's Stone in the Gower Peninsula in Wales. I am told that on Midsummer's Day each year a flash of light will be seen for just a moment under the stone and then not again until next Midsummer's Day. The boulder rests on pillars and is two metres high and is thought to have been constructed by Neolithic man. Its shadow, like a dial, marks the changing seasons by striking other stones in the Gower Peninsula, and in fact sometimes it is referred to as the Stonehenge of Wales.

Man always seems to have the ingenuity to capture those meaningful flashes of light, and one of the most memorable of those I found in the beautiful War Memorial in Melbourne, Australia. There is a Shrine of Remembrance and it is so designed that at exactly the eleventh hour of the eleventh day of the eleventh month a ray of light comes through the ceiling and shines on the word 'Love' in the inscription 'Greater Love Hath No Man Than This.' To pick out the word 'Love' from these words of Christ symbolises to me the very heart and light and life of the Gospel.

November 23rd

Samuel Becket once wrote that we should never despair, because the repentant thief was promised entry into Paradise. But neither should we presume, for there was no such promise for the unrepentant thief.

> When all within is dark
> and former friends misprise
> From them I turn to You
> And find love in your eyes.
>
> When all within is dark
> and I my soul despise
> From me I turn to You
> And find love in your eyes.
>
> When all your face is dark
> and your just angers rise
> From You I turn to You
> And find love in your eyes.

Ibn Gabirol (11th Century Spanish)

November 24th

> Love bade me welcome, yet my soul drew back,
>   Guilty of dust and sin.
> But quick-eyed Love, observing me grow slack
>   From my first entrance in,
> Drew nearer to me, sweetly questioning
>   If I lacked anything.
>
> 'A guest,' I answered, 'worthy to be here.'
>   Love said, 'You shall be he.'
> 'I, the unkind, ungrateful? Ah, my dear,
>   I cannot look on thee.'
> Love took my hand and smiling did reply,
>   'Who made the eyes but I?'

'Truth, Lord, but I have marred them; let my shame
    Go where it doth deserve.'
'And know you not,' says Love, 'who bore the blame?'
    'My dear, then I will serve.'
'You must sit down,' says Love, 'and taste my meat.'
    So I did sit and eat.

George Herbert

November 25th

The holiest of our holidays are those
Kept by ourselves in silence and apart
The secret anniversaries of the heart.

Longfellow

November 26th

There are people like Corrie Ten Boom who had so much to forgive the Nazis for because of their treatment of her family; and Eric Lomax who had so much to forgive the Japanese for because of their inhuman cruelty towards the prisoners in their camps. They both revealed the real hard task it is to forgive wholeheartedly. But there came a time when they each were face to face with their torturers and yet they found that such forgiveness was truly possible.

Corrie Ten Boom in talking about all our need for forgiveness from God for our sins, says: 'When God forgives our sins, he separates them as far from us as the east is from the west, buries them in the bottom of the deepest sea, and puts up a sign for the Devil - saying "NO FISHING!"'

November 27th

Praise the Lord, O my soul,
    all my inmost being, praise his holy name
Praise the Lord, O my soul,
    and forget not all his benefits -
who forgives all your sins
    and heals all your diseases,
who redeems your life from the pit
    and crowns you with love and compassion,
who satisfies your desires with good things
so that your youth is renewed as the eagle's.

The Lord is compassionate and gracious,
slow to anger, abounding in love.
He will not always accuse,
nor will he harbour his anger for ever,
he does not treat us as our sins deserve
Or repay us according to our iniquities.
For as high as the heavens are above the earth,
so great is his love for those that fear him;
as far as the east is from the west,
so far has he removed our transgressions from us.
As a father has compassion on his children,
so the Lord has compassion
on those who fear him.

Psalm 103: 1-5 & 8-13

November 28th

Almighty and tender Lord Jesus Christ,
I have asked you to be good to my friends,
and now I bring before you
what I desire in my heart for my enemies.

You alone, Lord, are mighty;
you alone are merciful;
whatever you make me desire for my enemies,
give it to them and give the same back to me,
and if what I ask at any time
is outside the rule of charity,
whether through weakness, ignorance, or malice,
good Lord, do not give it to them
and do not give it back to me.

You who are the true light, lighten their darkness;
you who are the whole truth, correct their errors;
you who are the true life, give life to their souls.

St. Anselm

November 29th

A woman in the East End of London was before the judge for contempt of court.

'Just make that "utter contempt!"' she scornfully addressed him.

She was a touch more feisty than the young lawyer to whom the Judge said, 'I think you are trying to show contempt for the court.'

'No, my Lord, I was merely trying to conceal it.'

November 30th

Say not the struggle naught availeth,
    The labour and the wounds are vain,
The enemy faints not, nor faileth,
    And as things have been they remain.

If hopes were dupes, fears may be liars;
    It may be, in yon smoke concealed,
Your comrades chase e'en now the fliers,
    And but for you possess the field.

For while the tired waves, vainly breaking,
    Seem here no painful inch to gain,
Far back, through creeks and inlets making
    Comes silent, flooding in, the main.

And not by eastern windows only,
    When daylight comes, comes in the light;
In front the sun climbs slow, how slowly,
    But westward, look, the land is bright!

A. H. Clough

THRESHOLD OF LIGHT

Meditations as we approach Christmas

Approaching Christmas (1)

A woman went into one of our big stores at Christmas time to try to get an illustrated children's Bible for one of her grand-children. She wasn't successful in her search of the shelves, so she asked an assistant for help. 'We do have them in the store,' said the assistant, 'but we had to clear them off the shelves to make way for the real children's Christmas books.' And she pointed out the abundance of material based on the latest TV personalities or puppets. So we can at times feel we are moving towards a Christmas without Christ, where the pressures of our commercial world are crowding out the real central story.

It is perhaps salutary before we start thinking deeply about Christ's coming to read again some of John Betjeman's words about Advent.

For now we feel the world spin round
On some momentous journey bound -
Journey to what? to whom? to where?
The Advent bells call out 'Prepare,
Your world is journeying to the birth
Of God made Man for us on earth.'

And how in fact do we prepare
For the great day that waits us there -
The twenty-fifth day of December,
The birth of Christ? For some it means
An interchange of hunting scenes
On coloured cards. And I remember
Last year I sent out twenty yards,
Laid end to end of Christmas cards
To people that I scarcely know -
They'd sent a card to me, and so
I had to send one back. Oh dear!
Is this a form of Christmas cheer?
Or is it, which is less surprising,
My pride gone in for advertising?
The only cards that really count
Are that extremely small amount

From real friends who keep in touch
And are not rich but love us much.
Some ways indeed are very odd
by which we hail the birth of God.

We raise the price of things in shops,
We give plain boxes fancy tops
And lines which traders cannot sell
Thus parcell'd go extremely well.
We dole out bribes we call a present
To those to whom we must be pleasant
For business reasons. Our defence is
These bribes are charged against expenses
And bring relief in Income Tax.
Enough of these unworthy cracks!

'The time draws near the birth of Christ'
A present that cannot be priced
Given two thousand years ago.
Yet if God had not given so
He still would be a distant stranger
And not the Baby in the manger.

Approaching Christmas (2)

I read the other day about a New Zealand mother who was expecting her third child, and was facing difficulties because it was a breech birth. Her doctor on the occasion was Jewish, and she said to him, 'Please, whatever happens, take great care of the baby.'

'Of course I will,' he said gently, 'I take great care of every baby I deliver. Any one of them might be the Messiah.'

It is not difficult to transfer the emotions of that expectant mother, and indeed the emotions and care of the doctor, to Mary and also to Joseph as they pondered the news that the baby they were to care for was the Promised One. The message had been given to Mary that she was to bear the Christ. For those of us who have difficulty with the virgin birth, it is salutary to note that Mary herself was the first to say, 'How can these things be?' Only Matthew and Luke go into detail about the birth, and I have no great difficulty with this either or with the fact that the four Gospels and indeed the whole of the New Testament present different aspects of the life and teaching of Christ. If you have ever taken a class of children out of the classroom for a new experience and then asked them to write about it afterwards, the accounts would be as varied as the personalities involved. But they will all be recognised as true accounts though each emphasising different experiences.

Luke's account is much fuller than Matthew's, maybe because he was a doctor, and with a warm interest in people. Perhaps much of the account he gives comes direct from Mary and possibly some from Joseph as well.

The very important central truth is that this event is of significance to the entire world. God broke into his own world and came among us.

> God all-bounteous, all creative
> Whom no ills from good dissuade,
> Is incarnate and a native
> Of the very world he made.
>
> *Christopher Smart*

Approaching Christmas (3)

When my youngest grandchild was nearly three he loved to have the nursery tales read and re-read to him. One night when I was going through them again he stopped me and said, 'Don't say Goldilocks and don't say Pinocchio. Say Jonathan instead.' So each time, I would substitute his name for the nursery character and he would accurately repeat the words they would have spoken at the given time in the tale. It was very obvious that like Peter Pan, he was saying, 'Can I be in this story?' When Christmas comes with all its wonderful repetitions of the different happenings, it is good to pause and ask ourselves, 'Am I in this story and what does it really mean to me?'

If we take Matthew and Luke together there are two astonishing lists of those who are in the story even though they lived before the birth. Matthew shows Jesus as descended from Abraham through the line of David as far as Joseph, to whom Mary was betrothed. To me there must be some significance in those listed, for the wideness of God's grace is such that amongst the list are Tamar who had children by her father-in-law Judah; Rahab who was a Jericho prostitute; and Ruth who was an alien Moabite. There was also Uriah's wife, Bathsheba, with whom David committed adultery. The Bible is a very honest book indeed.

Sometimes we just skip over these long lists, but at Christmas it is valuable to study the fact that Matthew and Luke wanted recorded the lineage of Joseph. We make much of Mary being the chosen mother, and rightly so. But wasn't the choice of Joseph to be her espoused important also? Luke gives his list later in the unfolding of the story of Jesus' life. His list goes back to Adam. He considers it important to note all those names but he chose the time of reporting to coincide with Jesus' baptism in the Jordan followed by the descent of the Holy Spirit in the shape of a dove. All those in the story up until Christ's birth were like all mankind today - in need of a Messiah, a Redeemer. God and man are united in the Saviour God chose to call his beloved son.

When God Almighty came to be one of us,
Masking the glory of his golden train,
Dozens of plain things happened by accident,
And they will never be the same again.
Sing all you midwives, dance all you carpenters,
Sing all the publicans and shepherds too,
God in his mercy uses the commonplace,
God on his birthday had a need of you.

Michael Hewlett

Approaching Christmas (4)

When Fynn wrote the extraordinary story of Anna in Mister God, This Is Anna, he has her making some strange statements. She liked best to be in church alone so that she could dance there for Mister God. She said she was bothered that people seemed to go to church to look for miracles, whereas for Anna everything was a miracle and the greatest miracle was that she was living in it.

There were those around at the time of Christ's nativity who realised that a miracle was happening and that they were living in it. Zechariah was in Jerusalem performing his priestly duties when it was revealed to him that he and his wife Elizabeth would have a son who would be the forerunner of the Lord, the Messiah. That was a miracle in itself, confirmed after Mary, espoused to Joseph had her revelation which she confided to Elizabeth.

That journey of Mary from Nazareth to Elizabeth in her hill town of Judaea must have taken four or five days - a tiring journey for a pregnant and bewildered girl.

Their meeting was so joyful and significant that we have some of the most beautiful of all Scriptures in Elizabeth's words of benediction and humility. 'Why am I so favoured that the mother of my Lord should come to me?' These words are followed by the exquisite words we now call The Magnificat. And then we have the simple statement that Mary stayed with Elizabeth for about three months and then returned home. Can you imagine the conversations between those two special mothers-to-be? Those of us who have known the miracle of a normal pregnancy and birth ourselves can enter into something of the sense of wonder, the feelings of awe, the waiting, the hopes, the fears, the joys. I like to think of the words which Luke used later of Mary and I use them also in my imagination as she left Elizabeth and journeyed back to her own house. She would have 'kept all these things and pondered them in her heart.'

> Joy to the world, the Lord is come
> Let earth receive her king
> Let every heart prepare him room
> And heaven and nature sing.
>
> *Isaac Watts*

Approaching Christmas (5)

At this time of year, schools and churches all over the world will be preparing their own version of the Nativity scene. The very first attempt at arranging a manger scene is supposed to have been made in 1224 by Francis of Assissi. Near the little town of Greccio coming up to Christmas he saw some shepherds lying asleep in the fields, and this reminded him so much of the Christmas story that he decided to create a nativity scene which would enable the ordinary peasant folk to get a picture of what the very first Christmas might have been like.

He made a crèche and placed it out in the forest with a real ox and ass tethered nearby. Real people represented the Holy Family and the shepherds, and the villagers came to sing their praise. Of course, we can understand that the event would be repeated annually thereafter, and the idea spread throughout Italy and to other countries throughout Europe and later other parts of the world.

I have heard a few cynics scorn this type of representation, but I know from experiencing the preparation with children how illuminating such a scene can become for children and adult alike. The one safeguard I like to keep is that the Bible story should be read again as it is really declared to us. Though we may illuminate parts of it with legend it is necessary to separate out the two.

Bethlehem was indeed royal David's city and to me it is a touching fact that David was a shepherd boy once. And the first to be told the good news of the arrival of the Messiah were humble shepherds, keeping watch over their flocks. I associate them with that earlier chosen shepherd, David, and the words from Psalm 78: vs 70 -72

> He chose David his shepherd
> and took him from the sheep pens;
> From tending the sheep he brought him
> to be the shepherd of his people Jacob,
> of Israel his inheritance.
> And David shepherded them with integrity of heart:
> with skilful hands he led them.

The shepherds chosen to be told of Jesus' birth had integrity of heart also for it must have been their first-hand story which was related to the Gospel writer and accepted as true.

....

I shall never forget approaching our first Christmas after my husband had died prematurely. I was teaching a class of youngsters and telling them the story of Christ being laid in a manger, and was about to relate how the shepherds got the news from the host of angels that they must journey to Bethlehem. I had started to say, 'And then the angel said......' when quite spontaneously the class recited in unison the words, 'For behold I bring you good tidings of great joy, which shall be to all people. For unto you is born this day, in the city of David, a Saviour which is Christ the Lord.'

It is difficult to describe what that little incident meant to me at that particular time when my personal grief was raw. The real meaning of that first Christmas with the coming of the one whose name was Emmanuel, 'God with us' came with a kind of heavenly radiance and an assurance of goodwill and peace. Let us rest in this truth at this joyous season.

Though Christ a thousand times
In Bethlehem be born,
If he's not born in thee
Thy soul is still forlorn.

Angelus Silesius

Approaching Christmas (6)

One of the sites of Israel which shall always stand out in my mind is the isolated desert mountain of Masada, looming some 1400 feet above the Dead Sea. Why should I think of it now when we are approaching Christmas? It is the place where some seven decades after Christ's birth, and after the fall of Jerusalem, the zealots took up their last stance of resistance against the Tenth Roman Legion. The oration of El Azar to those under seige is moving even today not only to the Jews who visit there, but also to those of us who are not Jews. Part of that oration says,'Pity the young whose bodies are strong enough to survive torture; pity the not-so-young whose old frames would break under such ill-usage.' In the end three hundred and sixty men, women and children died rather than fall into Roman captivity. What has this to do with Christmas?

This very stronghold where they died at Masada had earlier been built by the Herod who was king when Christ was born. The Herods were known for their streak of cruelty. This Herod was the same who was visited by the Magi, the astrologers who had been following the star looking for a king. Herod's cruelty was manifested because of his jealousy of the baby who was likely to be a rival king. He ordered the ruthless slaughter of the innocents in Bethlehem, when he realised that the Magi had outwitted him. It is poignant to think the massacre took place where the angels sang their song of peace on earth. We cannot just remember the cosy winsome part of the Christmas story without paying some attention to the pain.

The story of the Magi is only told by Matthew and no mention of three characters is made, but because the three gifts were described, it is fairly safe to assume they were three. In our nativity plays we concertina the events and have the Magi arriving at the stable, but Matthew speaks of them being in a house, which indicates a later time, especially when the slaughter ordered by Herod was to be of all boys under two years old.

Many beautiful legends have been developed, enlarging on Matthew's story, and about the sixth century the Magi came to be described as kings, and are usually so depicted in our nativity plays. The gifts of course are symbolic: gold was given as a tribute to Christ the king: frankincense related to his divinity: and myrrh, standing for suffering, foretold his death.

We might ponder at this time the strange link between the three gifts and the words used by Mary in the Magnificat: 'My soul doth magnify the Lord, and my spirit hath rejoiced in God my Saviour' - *our Lord and king: our God: our Saviour*

What can I give him
Poor as I am?
If I were a shepherd
I would bring a lamb.
If I were a wise man
I would do my part
But what I can I give him
Give my heart.

Christina Rossetti

CHRISTMAS AND THE WISE MEN

The offerings of the Eastern kings of old
Unto our Lord, were incense, myrrh and gold;
Incense because a God: gold as a king;
And myrrh as to a dying man they bring.
Instead of incense, Blessed Lord, if we
Can send a fervent prayer to thee,
Instead of myrrh if we can but provide
Tears that from penitential eyes do slide,
And though we have no gold, if for our part
We can present you with a broken heart
You will accept: and say those Eastern kings
Did not present you with more precious things.

Nathaniel Wanley

CHRISTMAS BELLS

I heard the bells on Christmas Day
Their old familiar carols play,
    And wild and sweet
    The words repeat
Of 'Peace on earth, goodwill to men.'

And in despair I bowed my head;
'There is no peace on earth,' I said
    'For hate is strong
    and mocks the song
Of peace on earth, goodwill to men.'

Then pealed the bells more loud and deep:
'God is not dead, nor doth he sleep!
    The wrong shall fail
    The right prevail,
With peace on earth, goodwill to men.'

Henry Wadsworth Longfellow

DECEMBER

The sky turns dark, the year grows old,
The buds draw in before the cold.

Theodore Roethke

December 1st

I cannot tell why he whom angels worship,
should set his love upon the sons of men,
or why as Shepherd, he should seek the wanderers,
to bring them back, they know not where or when.
But this I know, that he was born of Mary,
when Bethlehem's manger was his only home,
and that he lived at Nazareth and laboured,
and so the Saviour, Saviour of the world is come.

I cannot tell how silently he suffered,
as with his peace he graced the place of tears,
or how his heart upon the cross was broken,
the crown of pain to three and thirty years.
But this I know, he heals the broken hearted,
and stays our sin, and calms our lurking fear,
and lifts the burden from the heavy laden,
for yet the Saviour, Saviour of the world, is here.

I cannot tell how he will win the nations,
how he will claim his earthly heritage,
how satisfy the needs and aspirations
of east and west, of sinner and of sage.
But this I know, all flesh shall see his glory,
and he shall reap the harvest he has sown,
and some glad day his sun shall shine in splendour
when he the Saviour, Saviour of the world, is known.

I cannot tell how all the lands shall worship,
when at his bidding, every storm is stilled,
or who can say how great the jubilation
when all the hearts of men with love are filled.
But this I know, the skies will fill with rapture,
and myriad, myriad human voices sing,
and earth to heaven, and heaven to earth will answer:
At last the Saviour, Saviour of the world is King!

William Young Fullerton

December 2nd

C.S. Lewis wrote an article called The Grand Miracle in which he deals with the miracle of the entire Christian story from Christ's birth to his resurrection. In writing about the events leading up to the Nativity he says of God's Chosen People, the Jews, 'One people picked out of the whole earth; that people purged and proved again and again. Some are lost in the desert before they reach Palestine; some stay in Babylon; some becoming indifferent. The whole thing narrows and narrows, until at last it comes down to a little point, small as a point of a spear - a Jewish girl at her prayers.'

December 3rd

This is the month, and this the happy morn,
Wherein the Son of heaven's eternal King
Of wedded maid and virgin mother born,
Our great redemption from above did bring;
For so the holy sages once did sing,
That he our deadly forfeit should release,
And with his Father work us a perpetual peace.

John Milton

December 4th

All over the world little children will at this time of the month be preparing for taking part in their own version of the Nativity. In one village school the parents as usual were being asked to help in the provision of makeshift costumes, and all the old sheets for the angels and old dressing gowns for the kings and toy lambs for the shepherds were being gathered in. One baffled parent arrived at the school asking for clarification as to what she was expected to provide for her little five-year-old boy, who maintained adamantly that all he needed was a piece of paper.

'What exactly is Peter playing in the Nativity play?' the mother asked.

'He is to be a page,' replied the teacher.

December 5th

At this overly busy time of the year for most of us it might be good to read the following.

I got up early one morning
and rushed right into the day
I had so much to accomplish
that I did not have time to pray.

Problems just tumbled about me
and heavier came each task
'Why doesn't God help me?' I wondered.
He answered, 'You didn't ask!'

I wanted to see joy and beauty
but the day toiled on, grey and bleak
I wondered why God didn't show me
He said, 'You didn't seek!'

I tried to come into God's presence
I used all my keys at the lock
God gently and lovingly chided
'My child, you didn't knock!'

I woke up early this morning
and *paused* before starting the day
I had so much to accomplish
I just *had* to take time to pray.

Unattributed

December 6th

When Mary was told that she was the one chosen to give birth to the Messiah, Matthew tells us that she left immediately and went into the hills of Judah. I like to think that she might in her bewilderment have repeated to herself Psalm 121, as it was evident that she was familiar with the Scriptures.

I will lift up my eyes to the hills -
  where does my help come from?
My help comes from the Lord,
  the Maker of heaven and earth.

He will not let your foot slip -
  he who watches over you will not slumber;
indeed, he who watches over Israel
  will neither slumber nor sleep.

The Lord watches over you -
    the Lord is your shade at your right hand;
the sun will not harm you by day,
    nor the moon by night.

The Lord will keep you from all harm -
    he will watch over your life;
the Lord will watch over your coming and going
    both now and for evermore.

Psalm 121

December 7th

Holy Spirit, think through me
    till your ideas are my ideas.

It is not far to go
    for you are near
It is not far to go
    for you are here.
And not by travelling, Lord,
    men come to you,
But by the way of love
    and we love you.

Amy Carmichael

December 8th

SAFE OR SORRY ?

The geese which did not fly enjoyed
    the sunlit farmyard
    the calm pond
    the regular and plentiful food (for which they
        clamoured)
    the shelter from rain and cold
    the protection from *most* dangers.

They did not do much
    but were good at making great noise
They did not fly, these geese
They never knew
    the exhilaration of something dared
    the wild pressure of wind and rain
    the comfort of the drying sun
    the challenge of danger
    the wisdom to hunt for food
    and the wit to leave the farmyard.

The farmyard geese missed
those who were not there next morning.
most often at Christmas.
Then came a tiny worry
that maybe the farmyard
was not so safe
or so satisfying
after all!

Unattributed

December 9th

I have used before some of the sayings of Archy the cockroach who was the constant companion of the writer Don Marquis. Archy was given to having random thoughts and one of them was: 'I have noticed that when chickens quit quarrelling over their food they find that there is enough for all of them. I wonder if it might not be the same way for the human race.'

This is a salutary thought during this month of feasting and drinking for most of us whilst there is still so much famine in the world.

December 10th

I saw a stable, low and very bare,
A little child in a manger.
The oxen knew him, had him in their care,
To men he was a stranger.
The safety of the world was lying there,
And the world's danger.

Mary Coleridge

December 11th

This is the time of year when we all have to study our bank balances carefully so that we do not go overboard spending foolishly on extravagances. Here is an amusing tale.

A banker and an insurance broker went up on a balloon voyage and ran out of gas and came down on top of a very high tree. A man passed by underneath and they asked them if he could tell them exactly where they were.

'Yes,' he answered, 'You are stuck in the branches of a very high tree, in a balloon.'

'That man must be an accountant,' said the banker. 'You ask a perfectly sensible and simple question and he gives a perfectly accurate and useless answer.'

December 12th

For sheer delight of tasting once again
The first crisp breath of winter in the air:
The pictured pane: the now white world without:
The sparkling hedgerows witchery of lace,
The soft white flakes that fold the sleeping earth:
The cold without, the cheerier warmth within . . . .
For all the glowing heart of Christmastide
We thank you, Lord.

John Oxenham

December 13th

The people walking in darkness
    have seen a great light
on those living in the land of the shadow of death
    a light has dawned.

For to us a child is born,
    to us a son is given,
    and the government will be on his shoulders.
And he will be called
    Wonderful Counsellor, Mighty God,
Everlasting Father, Prince of Peace.
Of the increase of his government and peace
    there will be no end.

Isaiah 9: 2 & 6-7

December 14th

Lord, we are perplexed as we consider again the message of peace and goodwill at this festive time, for we realise how far short we have fallen in achieving a peaceful world. Help us to see the human predicament as you see it and to recognise afresh what you meant by sending your Son for our salvation. Give us new hope this Christmastide that the true way of reconciliation in all parts of your torn world may be found. We are so divided and you came to bring us unity.

Forgive our stubbornness and enable us by your love to break down wherever we can the barriers of hatred. Prince of Peace, by the power of your Spirit, bring us true peace.

December 15th

I remember during the Second World War a plea was made through Parliament that Chamberlain, the Prime Minister of the day, should set aside a day for prayer for the end of the war. Chamberlain's answer was that the matter would be considered *at the proper time.* 'I do not think that time has arrived,' he said. A New York paper made a very pertinent and stinging statement about this response.

> 'This remark we feel represents the ultimate in British caution. The Prime Minister has apparently an uneasy faith in the power of prayer combined with a lack of faith in the Divine grasp of the situation. Pray for the end of the war and there is a chance that is what you will get; peace right on the dot with all the issues right up in the air and the balance of power yet to be determined. The Prime Minister it seems has no doubt that God can put a stop to hostilities any time he feels like it, but he would rather not trust him with the details. The time for peace will be determined at 10 Downing Street. Until the Cabinet gives the word, the people will kindly refrain from stirring up the Divine. Until the Empire has things better under control, God can just count sparrows.'

So what about families who are at war with each other? I read a frightening statistic recently which stated that research had shown that family stress counsellors were consulted most frequently after family holidays and family Christmases. Perhaps more than at any other season people are attempting happy family reunions at Christmas just because it's a tradition. And maybe they're battling against a background of personal hostility or alienation.

It may be necessary to stir up the Divine. We must give him credit for having knowledge of each situation and not just leave him to count sparrows. He can in truth bring peace if we but allow him room but sometimes the healing of old wounds is a painful and humbling process.

December 16th

> The soul that has believed
> And is deceived
> Thinks nothing for a while
> All thoughts are vile.

And then because the sun is mute persuasion
And hope in Spring or Fall most natural

The soul grows calm and mild
A little child
Finding the pull of breath
Better than death.

The soul that had believed
And was deceived
Ends by believing more
Than ever before.

Virginia Moore

December 17th

The sophistication of modern youngsters can give a very diifferent version of the Christmas story. One pupil was asked how it was that Mary got the news that she was about to have a baby boy. She answered without hesitation, 'Well, I expect she had been for her scan.'

They were all looking for a king
To slay their foes and lift them high
Thou cam'st a little baby thing
That made a woman cry.

George MacDonald

December 18th

End of term in colleges and universities at Christmas can be a time of special rejoicing and jollification because there is some respite from what can sometimes be tedious lectures and tedious lecturers.

Of all the kinds of lecturer
The lecturer I most detest
Is he who finishes a page
And places it behind the rest.

I much prefer the lecturer
Who takes the pages as he finishes
And puts them in a mounting pile
As the original pile diminishes.

But best of all the lecturer
Who gets his papers in confusion
And prematurely lets escape
The trumpet phrase - 'And in conclusion......'

December 19th

Gwen Dunn wrote a long poem about a little boy called Tim whose job it was to fetch the hay for the manger where Baby Jesus was to lie. After he fetched it from the pet shop he said,

> 'You'd think they could have found
> Something better than hay
> For a new-born King
> On a winter's day!'

December 20th

> Sing to God, sing praise to his name,
> extol him who rides on the clouds -
> his name is the Lord -
> and rejoice before him.
> A father to the fatherless, a defender of widows,
> is God in his holy dwelling.
> God sets the lonely in families
> he leads forth the prisoners with singing.

Psalm 68: 4-6

December 21st

> O Lord,
> Open my eyes that I may see the needs of others;
> Open my ears that I may hear their cries;
> Open my heart so that they need not be without succour;
> Let me not be afraid to defend the weak because of the anger of the strong,
> nor afraid to defend the poor because of the anger of the rich.
> Show me where love and hope and faith are
> and use me to bring them to those places.
> And so open my eyes and my ears so that I may this coming day
> be able to do some work of peace for you.

Alan Paton

December 22nd

WHAT THE DONKEY SAW

No room in the inn, of course,
And not that much in the stable,
What with the shepherds, Magi, Mary,
Joseph, the heavenly host -
Not to mention the baby
Using our manger as a cot.
You couldn't have squeezed another cherub in
For love nor money.

Still, in spite of the overcrowding,
I did my best to make them feel wanted.
I could see the baby and I
Would be going places together.

U.A. Fanthorpe

December 23rd

It was time for the school Nativity drama. Young Joseph in the five year old class was having some difficulty in deciding how to look after Mary properly when he led her to the manger. His teacher said, 'You know when your own Mummy gets tired and your Daddy tries to help her. Just do as he would do.'

Immediate enlightenment seemed to dawn. Briskly Joseph moved towards Mary and said with no hesitation at all, 'Just put your feet up here, dear, and I'll soon fix you a gin and tonic.'

December 24th

REINDEER REPORT

Chimneys: colder.
Flightpaths: busier.
Driver: Christmas (F)
Still baffled by postcodes.

Children: more
and stay up later.
Presents: heavier.
Pay: frozen.

Mission in spite
Of all this
Accomplished.

U.A. Fanthorpe

December 25th

Come, worship the King
That little white thing
Asleep on his mother's soft breast
Ye bright stars bow down
Weave for him a crown
Christ Jesus by angels confessed.

Come, children and peep
But hush ye, and creep
On tiptoe to where the Babe lies;
Then whisper his name
And lo! like a flame
The glory light shines in his eyes.

Come, strong men and see
This high mystery
Tread firm where the shepherds have trod,
And watch, 'mid the hair
Of the maiden so fair
The five little fingers of God.

Come, old men and grey
The star leads the way
It halts and your wanderings cease;
Look down on his face
Then filled with his grace
Depart ye, God's servants, in peace.

Studdert Kennedy

December 26th

Many years back, the following passage was printed anonymously in a paper published in Hamilton, Ontario. It was copied in some of our papers and used on many occasions since.

ONE SOLITARY LIFE

Here is a man who was born of Jewish parents in an obscure village, the child of a peasant woman. He grew up in another obscure village. He worked in a carpenter's shop until he was thirty, and then for three years he was an itinerant preacher.

He never wrote a book, he never held an office, he never owned a home. He never had a family. He never went to college.

He never travelled two hundred miles from the place where he was born. He never did one of these things that usually accompany greatness. He had no credentials but himself.

He had nothing to do with this world except the naked power of his manhood. While still a young man, the tide of popular opinion turned against him. His friends ran away. One of them denied him. He was turned over to his enemies. He went through the mockery of a trial.

He was nailed to a cross between two thieves. His executioners gambled for the only piece of property he had on earth, while he was dying - and that was his coat. When he was dead he was taken down and laid in a borrowed grave, through the pity of a friend.

Nineteen *(now twenty)* wide centuries have come and gone, and today he is the centrepiece of the human race, and the leader of the column of progress. I am far within the mark when I say that all the armies that ever marched, and all the navies that were ever built, and all the parliaments that ever sat, and all the kings that ever reigned, put together, have not affected the life of man upon earth as powerfully as has that solitary life.

December 27th

Dear friends, let us love one another, for love comes from God. Everyone who loves has been born of God and knows God. Whoever does not love does not know God, because God is love. This is how God has showed his love among us. He sent his one and only Son into the world that we might live through him. This is love: not that we loved God, but that he loved us and sent his Son for an atoning sacrifice for our sins. Dear friends, since God so loved us, we also ought to love one another. No-one has ever seen God, but if we love one another, God lives in us and his love is made complete in us.

We know that we live in him and he in us, because he has given us of his Spirit. And we have seen and testify that the Father has sent his Son to be the Saviour of the world.

1 John 4: 7-14

December 28th

Lord and Saviour,
As this year draws to its close,
we bring it to you - every day of it.
All the days of fulfilment and achievement
All the days of failure and disappointment
the days full of sorrow
the days enhanced by joy
the days we wasted in forgetfulness of you
the days which were enriched by your presence
Take this imperfect tapestry which we present to you at this year's close
and by your grace cleanse and remove from it all unpleasing in your sight.
Now help us go forward in your strength and love and peace
For your mercy's sake Amen.

December 29th

There are times when we can never meet the future with sufficient elasticity of mind, especially if we are locked in the contemporary systems of thought. We can do worse than remember a principle which both gives us a firm Rock and leaves us the maximum elasticity of our minds: the principle: Hold to Christ, and for the rest be totally uncommitted.

Herbert Butterfield

With every power for good to stay and guide me,
Comforted and inspired beyond all fear,
I'll live these days with you in thought beside me,
And pass, with you, into the coming year.

Dietrich Bonhoeffer

December 30th

And now, a little mirth.

The taxi driver at Waverley Street Station, Edinburgh, saw an affluent looking American approach his rank and as it was the festive season he looked forward to a rewarding fare enhanced by a lavish tip. His hopes were raised even higher when the American said to him, 'Do you know the bonny bonny banks of Loch Lomond?' Well, of course he did.

'Then whistle it to me as you drive me to Murrayfield,' blithely requested the American.

December 31st

As we enter a New Year and go further into a new century I have been pondering 1 John 4: 12-14 which gives us a neat encapsulation of the doctrine of the Trinity. I wrote this hymn based on John's words. It can be sung to the favourite tune Blaenwern written by William Penfro Rowlands in the early part of the 20th century.

God Eternal, from all ages
Never seen by humankind
Yet within us you have promised
Light and meaning to the mind.
God unseen, yet we can know you
Reigning o'er each human heart,
Teaching us to love each other,
In your world we have a part.

Unseen God, you sent a Saviour,
Saviour of the world, your Son,
So we know you and we worship;
Your redemptive work is done.
When Christ rose beyond his dying,
Unseen God again you came,
Came to comfort, came to strengthen,
Holy Spirit, Heavenly flame.

Father, Son and Holy Spirit,
God unseen, yet God revealed;
Through the ages you have helped us;
Sins forgiven, bodies healed
By your Spirit freely given
You to us have truth unfurled;
As we face an unknown future
Help us claim you for our world.

Unseen God and unseen future
Come together now, we pray;
In our hearts we bid both welcome
As we journey day by day.
Trusting you for all that's needed
As in ages past supplied;
Joy, peace, faith, hope, love and wonder
Seen in Christ the crucified.

JOY BE WITH US

Joy be with us, and honour close the tale
Now do we dip the prow, and shake the sail
And take the wind and bid adieu to rest
With glad endeavour we begin the quest
That destiny commands, though where we go
Or by what star, no man can know.

James Stephens

May the door of the coming year open for you to Peace, Happiness and Quiet Contentment.

FINIS

Time present and time past
Are both perhaps present in time future
And time future contained in time past
T.S. Eliot (Four Quartets)

May the raindrops fall lightly
    on your brow
May the soft winds freshen
    your spirit
May the sunshine brighten
    your heart
May the burdens of the day
    rest lightly upon you
And may God fold you
    in the mantle of his love.

INDEX OF PRAYERS

Quarles, Francis	*March 21st*
Rossetti, Christina	*June 14th, July 7th, October 28th, Christmas (6)*
Ramsay, Malcolm	*January 14th, Easter Day, April 21st, August 15th*
Spitta, Karl J.B.	*September 21st*
Temple, William	*November 21st*
Toplady, Augustus M.	*October 23rd*
Urch, Michael	*October 14th, November 14th*
Wesley, Charles	*September 28th*
Wesley, John	*August 14th*
Whittier, John Greeleaf	*February 7th*
Wordsworth, Christopher	*July 13th*
Yom Kippur (Jewish)	*October 1st*

Other prayers have been composed by Elizabeth Urch

ACKNOWLEDGMENTS

I gratefully acknowledge permission to use copyright material. Thanks are recorded to those listed below. In some instances, despite my best endeavours I have been unable to find the source of some pieces or the executors of some authors. If any new information comes to light, redress will be made.

Bell, John and Maule, Graham: 'Take this moment' from "Love From Below": (Wild Goose Publications 1989) Copyright (c) 1989 Iona Community, 840 Govan Road, Glasgow, G51 3UU Scotland.

Betjeman, Sir John: 'Advent' The late Sir John, his executors and John Murray, Publishers.

Eliot, T.S.: 'Time present and time past' from 'Burnt Norton': Four Quartets, Faber and Faber Ltd.

Fanthorpe, U.A: 'Reindeer Report' and 'What The Donkey Saw': Peterloo Poets, 2 Kelly Gardens, Calstock, Cornwall, PL18 9SA.

Grenfell, Joyce: 'If I should go before the rest of you' from "Joyce Grenfell - by herself and friends" published by MacMillan London Ltd. and edited by Reggie Grenfell and Richard Garnett. (c) The Joyce Grenfell Memorial Trust 1980.

Lewis, C.S.: 'The Apologist's Evening Prayer' Harper Collins, Publishers.

Masefield, John: Extract from 'The Everlasting Mercy': The Society of Authors as the literary representative of the Estate of John Masefield.

Stephens, James: 'Joy Be With Us' The Society of Authors as the Literary Representative of the Estate of James Stephens.

Thomas R.S.: 'Life is not hurrying on to a receding future' from 'The Bright Field': R.S. Thomas and MacMillan Publishers.

Parabola Magazine: Yom Kippur Prayer: Parabola Magazine, New York.

Ramsay, Malcolm: 'What Language Shall They Borrow?' and prayers on January 14th, Easter Day and April 21st. Malcolm Ramsay, Pitlochry, Scotland.

Urch, Michael: 'Prayer For The Sorrowing' and prayer on October 14th. Michael Urch, Finland.